Cancer and Healing

To: Tracy Woods

I have Not allowed God's word to speak through me in regards to your painful lost of your brother, Jr. Main, & mother (Nae).

Please read these words with me even though God decided to our relatives home.

Curtis

MERCER
UNIVERSITY PRESS

Endowed by
TOM WATSON BROWN
and
THE WATSON-BROWN FOUNDATION, INC.

Cancer and Healing

Memoirs of Gratitude and Hope

Edited by

Charles W. Deweese

Mercer University Press
Macon, Georgia

MUP/P450

© 2012 Mercer University Press
1400 Coleman Avenue
Macon, Georgia 31207

First Edition

Royalties from the sale of this book will be donated to the American Cancer Society.

Books published by Mercer University Press are printed on acid-free paper that meets the requirements of American National Standard for Information Sciences—Permanence of Paper for Printed Library Materials.

Mercer University Press is a member of Green Press Initiative (greenpressinitiative.org), a nonprofit organization working to help publishers and printers increase their use of recycled paper and decrease their use of fiber derived from endangered forests. This book is printed on recycled paper.

Library of Congress Cataloging-in-Publication Data
    Cancer and healing : memoirs of gratitude and hope / edited by Charles W. Deweese. -- 1st ed.
        p. cm.
    Includes index.
    ISBN 978-0-88146-343-9 (hardback : alk. paper) -- ISBN 0-88146-343-4 (hardback : alk. paper) -- ISBN 978-0-88146-344-6 (e-book) -- ISBN 0-88146-344-2 (e-book)
    1. Baptists—Religious life. 2. Baptists—Biography. 3. Cancer—Patients—Religious life. 4. Cancer—Patients—Biography. I. Deweese, Charles W.
    BX6493.C35 2012
    248.8'6196994--dc22
                                                                    2011050961

Contents

Introduction

Soul-Jerking Journeys toward Healing

Charles W. Deweese
Retired Executive Director
Baptist History and Heritage Society

Cancer in all its viciousness and variety strikes almost 1.6 million people in the United States every year.[1] No two cancer victims' experiences are exactly the same. Everyone who suffers from and survives cancer has a different story to tell. In fact, "Medicine… begins with storytelling. Patients tell stories to describe illness; doctors tell stories to understand it. Science tells its own stories to explain diseases."[2]

Millions do not live to tell their stories. Almost 600,000 Americans and more than seven million people throughout the world die from cancer each year.[3] To help visualize that global number, try to think of seventy-plus football stadiums each filled with 100,000 people. Worldwide, this disease accounts for one in every eight deaths.[4] A microscopic disease that typically starts with a single, out-of-control cell, cancer is not choosy about whom it strikes, when it strikes, or what part of the body it strikes.

However, almost twelve million cancer survivors in the United States are celebrating birthdays this year because of

---

[1] *Cancer Facts & Figures 2011* (Atlanta: American Cancer Society, 2011) 1.

[2] Siddhartha Mukherjee, *The Emperor of All Maladies: A Biography of Cancer* (New York: Scribner, 2010) 390.

[3] Ibid., xi.

[4] *Cancer Facts & Figures 2011*, 45.

advancements in cancer research and treatment.[5] A recent study released by the Centers for Disease Control and Prevention concluded that one in twenty adults in America is a cancer survivor.[6] Still, "no simple, universal, or definitive cure is in sight" for cancer in general.[7]

Alexander Solzhenitsyn's novel *Cancer Ward* provided more than five hundred pages of massive detail regarding primitive treatment conditions rampant in a Soviet cancer hospital in the mid-1950s. Solzhenitsyn himself had received cancer treatment in such a setting. (That was the very decade in which I, as a child, witnessed the horrible cancer death of my own grandfather at his home in Asheville, North Carolina. He experienced excruciating pain from cancer that wracked his entire body.) Solzhenitsyn captured well the spirit of the cancer experience in the lives of many patients. In characterizing Vadim Zatsyrko, who had been diagnosed with a "melanoblastoma" and given eight months to live, he wrote: "This damn illness had cut right across his life, mowing him down at the crucial moment."[8] So today, there is much to be grateful for as treatments have advanced and research continues. While this disease continues to mow people down, millions of others survive and share their experiences.

Thomas Wolfe commented in his 1935 essay, "The Story of a Novel," that, "A man must use the material and experience of his own life if he is to create anything that has substantial value"[9] (Wolfe could have included women in that commentary

---

[5] Ibid., 1.

[6] Tyler Estep, "Study: One in 20 US adults is a cancer survivor," *Gwinnett Daily Post* (Lawrenceville GA), 16 March 2011, 12A.

[7] Mukherjee, *The Emperor of All Maladies*, 466.

[8] Alexander Solzhenitsyn, *Cancer Ward*, trans. from Russian (n.n.: The Bodley Head Ltd., 1968–69) 249.

[9] Cited in Thomas Wolfe, *You Can't Go Home Again*, HarperPerennial Modern Classics (New York: HarperCollins, 1998) 705.

on creativity). Nevertheless, at Wolfe's beckoning, this book moves inward. It lays out the personal cancer stories of ten men and eight women. But this book is not a fiction-based novel; it presents real experiences of real people. The writers live in ten states. Every person connected with this book, including the writers, editor, and university press director, has had and/or currently has cancer. The contributors have suffered multiple types of cancer and received a wide variety of treatments. All have reflected deeply on what has happened to them and what is happening. All thank every person who has ever ministered to them, and each expresses gratitude to God for healing and meaning and affirms hope for the future.

Autobiography, honestly written, can provide extraordinary insights into basic human dilemmas and achievements. Deliberate writings about oneself, including experiences, attitudes, and lessons, can penetrate deep into one's soul, share and shape one's identity, and expose one's vulnerabilities. While risky, such efforts at describing major challenges to life constitute the true stuff of a person's unimaginable circumstances. This book takes that risk, with all participants believing that while frank and open talk about a particular illness can get intensely personal, it can also minister helpfully to writers and readers who have to deal with cancer and its treatments.

By invitation, all participants in this publication agreed to bare their souls. So their very lives comprise the primary resources for this work. They have not written to make money; they have written for free. All royalties from sales of this book will be donated to the American Cancer Society. Writers selected for this project are all Baptists. Some are currently employed, while others are retired. Each contributor knows the suffering related to cancer and its treatment, but, more importantly, each has experienced gratitude and hope as a consequence of being forced to delve into that dark and difficult world.

3

What does it feel like to be told that one has cancer? What is it like to receive heavy doses of chemotherapy, or to undergo numerous radiation treatments, or to face multiple surgeries—or some combination of these and/or other treatments? How does one assess the meaning of life when faced with a disease that may or may not go into remission, and may or may not stay in remission? The autobiographical reflections presented in this book do not attempt to provide medical answers for such questions, but they do express a variety of personal feelings about critical life-and-death issues.

In one sense, the writers feel that we should keep our stories to ourselves. The stories are intensely personal and merit some privacy. However, we figure that sharing these stories may be good stewardship. We have learned a lot, and perhaps we can help someone deal with the sudden onslaught of cancer and its treatment. Contributors to this volume do not pretend that their experiences with cancer are any more traumatic than anyone else's; such pretense would be shameless. But the writers have experienced pain—physical, emotional, and spiritual—plus varying degrees of healing, gratitude, and hope.

The eighteen writers in this volume take different approaches to telling their stories. Some use humor; others do not. Some provide lots of details; others write more generally. Writers communicate in eighteen separate styles. Because the writers represent many types of Baptists, they apply many shades of theological meanings to their experiences.

Common denominators also apply. All writers express shock at hearing their doctors tell them that they have cancer. All find the maze of treatments to be initially overwhelming. All eventually find meaning in the treatments. All discover that cancer causes one to realize that some things can only take place "between God and me"; God becomes overwhelmingly personal and alive. All learn and share key lessons that evolve through their experiences. All are filled with gratitude and hope.

People have always sought deliverance from the onslaught of unwanted health problems both for themselves and for others. Betsey Lane was such a person. In 1893, Maine writer Sarah Orne Jewett published her short story, "The Flight of Betsey Lane," which told the story of an aging woman who lived on a poor-farm, Byfleet Farm, on the coast of Maine in the late 1800s. Through a gift of money from a friend, Betsey traveled to the Centennial Exposition in Philadelphia in 1876. There, she met a doctor whom she invited to the poor-farm to assist her vision-impaired friend, Peggy Bond. In the course of the conversation, Betsey told the doctor, "Most of us to the Byfleet Farm has got our ails, now I tell ye. You ain't got no bitters that'll take a dozen years right off an ol' lady's shoulders?"[10]

Once, while standing in a drug store in front of a shelf offering a variety of headache medicines, I overheard someone say, "We all got pains, ain't we?" I looked to my right, and there stood a tall, elderly woman. She, too, was looking at pain medicines. I chuckled and replied, "Yes, I guess we do." The woman's presence revealed that she needed relief of some sort; so did mine. More importantly, her comment, publicly expressed, revealed live evidence, both of humanity's saga of finiteness and of a universal cry for help and a yearning for healing. This book deals with such a yearning. And it expresses gratitude and hope during the journey. Each writer shares the enthusiasm of the Psalmist: "I sought the Lord, and he answered me, and delivered me from my fears" (Ps 34:4 NRSV).

Mystery surrounds the cancer experience. Potential causes of cancer seem to be unlimited: genetics, environment, working

---

[10] Sarah Orne Jewett, "The Flight of Betsey Lane," in *Great American Short Stories from Hawthorne to Hemingway,* ed. Corinne Demas (New York: Barnes & Noble Books, 2004) 254.

conditions, lifestyle, cell phones, and other factors. A recent article, "Cancer-causing list grows by 8," cites the dangers of styrene, used to make foam coffee cups, and formaldehyde, used to make plywood, pressboard, and certain hair treatments.[11] What about the irony that certain scans and treatments that can contribute to discovery and healing can also cause cancer?[12] And what about the sheer cost of cancer treatment? It is high and requires excellent health insurance.[13] That issue compounds itself with the realization that millions of Americans do not have health insurance.

These kinds of issues raise the obvious question: Are the treatment risks and costs worth it? The contributors to this book have obviously concluded that the advantages of additional life far outweigh both. They remain grateful for the hundreds of millions of hours that have gone into cancer drug research, the technology that has characterized radiation developments, the vast training and commitment of medical and surgical oncologists and nurses, the availability of cancer institutes and hospitals, the caring love of family and friends, and the hope made possible through the Lord himself who promised: "I am with you always, to the end of the age" (Matt. 28:20 NRSV).

---

[11] Gardiner Harris, "Cancer-causing list grows by 8," *The Atlanta Journal-Constitution*, 11 June 2011, A2.

[12] Christopher Moore, "Why I 'Ration' Care," *Newsweek*, 2 November 2009, 13; Liz Szabo, "CT scan radiation linked to cancers, deaths," *USA Today*, 15 December 2009; Mary A Fischer, "New Miracle Drugs," *AARP Magazine*, November/December 2009, 63; Ranit Mishori, "Limit the Risks of Radiation," *Parade*, 23 May 2010, 23; "Medical Radiation Is a Growing Concern," *The Wall Street Journal*, 15 June 2010, D9; Melody Petersen, "Over Exposed," *Good Housekeeping*, July 2010, 145; "How Dangerous Are Body Scans?" *Newsweek*, 13 December 2010, 13.

[13] Mike Stobbe, "Cost of cancer treatment soars," *The Atlanta Journal-Constitution*, 11 May 2010, A6.

Read these stories. Learn from the experiences of these eighteen writers. We never know when the downs of life will strike or the ups will surge. But through it all, we can know that God loves us.

I, as editor, am deeply grateful to all the contributors to this publication. All the writers have graciously shared slices of their souls that affirm God's power to rain down bread from heaven (Exod. 16:4) and to become the bread of life (John 6:35). The writers have traveled perilous journeys, but you can now share in their victories. If you as reader should have an interest in communicating with one of the writers, please contact Mercer University Press; the Press will then decide whether to pass along your interests/questions to the author.

From Fear to Faith

Bob R. Agee
President Emeritus
Oklahoma Baptist University and
Retired Executive Director
International Association of Baptist Colleges and Universities

Few emotions compare to what you feel when a doctor walks into your hospital room and tells you that you have an illness for which there is no guaranteed cure and which likely will shorten your life. On 28 September 1990, that is exactly what happened to me.

To say the least, it was unexpected. I guess I had known for several months that something was going on inside me that was different from any physical feelings I had ever known. For months I had noticed that I bruised more easily and that when I got a scratch, it did not heal as fast. For several years, I had been running three miles a day four or five days per week, but after a two-month lay-off due to scheduling problems, I discovered that I could not run a lap without being totally out of breath. Even after several weeks back on the track, I could not regain strength or stamina. I chalked these problems up to the fact that I was over fifty years of age and maybe those were the kinds of things that happen to one who passes the half-century mark.

In August 1990, I made a trip to mainland China to sign a new agreement with Xinjiang University that would stabilize and strengthen Oklahoma Baptist University's (OBU's) relationship with that institution. While coming out of China, I got sick in Hong Kong, and for several weeks following could not seem to get back on my feet. I developed a persistent fever and an uncontrollable cough for which the doctor could not find a cause. My doctor put me in the hospital for tests. Following an extensive battery of examinations and evaluations, he decided to send me to the Baptist Hospital in Oklahoma City for a bone-marrow aspiration. Even then the pathologists could not seem to find what was causing my blood counts to be so low. They just knew that something was wrong.

Finally, the chief pathologist at Baptist Hospital, who happened to have a son at OBU (where I was president at the time), determined to identify the problem. He recognized some of the symptoms and decided to try a test for a very rare form of leukemia. Sure enough, that test proved positive. They discovered that I had hairy-cell leukemia and that it was in an advanced stage.

Hairy-Cell Leukemia and My Reactions to It

The oncologist who broke the news to me was not very encouraging. He told me that at least half of the people who contract this disease live less than three years. It is a form of cancer that destroys blood cells at the point of origin in the bone marrow and thus destroys the immune system. A person seldom dies from the leukemia itself but becomes so susceptible to other diseases and infections that one of these usually takes the life of the patient. He told me of some experiments being run with only slight improvement in life expectancy and recommended a treatment program that involved taking a form of chemotherapy three times per week.

Regular doses of Interferon, taken for up to one year was his choice of treatment. Because the doctor still could not determine the cause of the high fever and the chronic cough, he decided to put me on Indicin, a medicine that I was to later learn should never be given to a leukemia patient. The side effects of the two drugs were devastating. I began to bleed internally and had to receive several blood transfusions. My system did not tolerate the Interferon well at all, and I felt that I was continuing to deteriorate. The prospects of long-term survival did not look good.

For a person who has been healthy, energetic, and active all of his life, hearing the very word cancer or leukemia was like getting kicked in the pit of the stomach. The idea that my life would most likely be shortened by a disease for which there was no reliable cure really took the wind out of my sails.

Almost immediately several emotions kicked into gear. The first was shock and fear. What would happen to the quality of my life? Who would watch after my family? What effect would this bad news have on them? I was not and am not afraid of death; I settled that long ago when I put my faith in Jesus Christ as my Savior and Lord. But dying was another thing. I have never done that before—that is new territory. What was out there in front of me? As I went through the weeks of dramatic weight loss (twenty-seven pounds in thirty days), blood trans-fusions, loss of energy, a depth of indescribable nausea, and several other unpleasant experiences, I found these develop-ments to be very frightening. I cherish independence and the ability to go and do as I please. I am an outdoorsman who loves fishing, boating, the forests, and adventure. Was that all going to be a thing of the past?

The second emotion that surfaced quickly was a deep sense of the presence of God in my life. I am an ordained minister who felt the call to preach when I was seventeen years old. I became a pastor when I was eighteen and have been in the pulpit regularly for thirty-four years. I spent eighteen years as a pastor and then went to Union University (my alma mater) as dean of religious affairs and professor of practical studies in the Religion Department. During my years of teaching at Union University, I served as interim pastor in one church after another for seven years. During the first nine years of my presidency at OBU, I averaged speaking in fifty churches a year.

All of a sudden, I was faced with the haunting question: Did I really believe all of those things that I have told people about God over the years? God had been so good to me. He had blessed me with good health, with abundant energy and opportunity. My God was, by and large, a God of good times. Even though I had known death of loved ones and had some heartaches, my life had been marked by far more good than bad. Was my God big enough to handle cancer? Was he big enough to carry me through the sickness and possibly the dying? Within a few hours after the time the doctor walked out of the room, an overwhelming sense of peace settled on me. God did not tell me that I would get well. He just made it known to me that he would be there; come what may, we would handle whatever this disease would throw at me. From that moment on I knew that no matter how dark the valleys or how dreadful the ordeal, he would be there to carry me through.

A third emotion kicked in alongside the first two. Perhaps it is a reflex that comes from somewhere down deep. Something went off inside me that said, "We're going to fight this thing." I do not like to lose at anything. I decided that I might die but if I did, I would go down fighting. I determined that I would learn everything I could about leukemia and would not rest until I had explored every possibility and fought on every battleground I could find. If there was any way to lick this stuff, I was going to find it. I owed it to my wife and to my kids to do battle.

The strange thing was that all three of those emotions became a part of my prayer pilgrimage. When I prayed, I often found myself wandering back and forth among those three sets of feelings, fluctuating from fear to faith to fighting and back again.

The Lord has intervened in my life. When the first treatment process was going about as badly as anything could, a bizarre series of events occurred, all of which, I am convinced, represented the Lord's intervention in answer to a lot of prayers being prayed on my behalf. Within two weeks, three unrelated events pointed me in a new direction for treatment.

One day in mid-November, I received a note of encouragement from my oldest daughter who lives in Jackson, Tennessee. The note included a newspaper clipping from the *Jackson Sun* telling about a new drug being tested that was having a very positive effect on hairy-cell leukemia. Within a few days, I received a copy of a report from the *New England Journal of Medicine* that told of this same drug being tested in New York indicating it was proving to be very effective in treating hairy-cell leukemia. Some of our faculty from the School of Nursing had found the article in their research and sent the article to me. The very next week I received a phone call from a businessman in Muskogee, Oklahoma, who told me that he, too, had hairy-cell leukemia and that he had gone to M.D. Anderson Cancer Center in Houston and received an experimental drug called 2-CdA. He told me that he was in remission and feeling great. He gave me his doctor's name at the center and a phone number to reach her.

Immediately, I called the number he had given me. When I told the doctor's nurse my situation, she called the doctor, who left a meeting to come to the phone to talk with me. She was the most encouraging person I had talked with since the diagnosis and told me to get my oncologist in Oklahoma City to refer me to her. When I talked to my oncologist, he had never heard of the experimental drug and was not aware of the research being done. I asked him to refer me to M.D. Anderson, which he did by the next day.

The drug was in its experimental stage and was being tested at three cancer research centers in the United States. It was administered intravenously for seven straight days, twenty-four hours a day, after which the IV was removed and I began the waiting process. The treatment was administered in early December 1990. By February, the evidence suggested that the drug was working, and by May I was declared in complete remission.

It would be nice if I could report that I remained in remission after that time, but my pilgrimage has been marked by four reoccurrences of the disease. The good news is that progress continues to be made in developing effective treatments for the various forms of adult leukemia, particularly the chronic forms. With each reoccurrence (1997, 2001, 2004, and 2009), the doctors have been able to treat the disease and send it back into remission. I often say that I am alive today because of the prayers of God's people, the wonders of medical science, and the miracle working grace of God.

In April 2007, I suffered a near-fatal heart attack in which I went into cardiac arrest four times over a two-hour period. Fortunately, the emergency medical technicians responded promptly to my wife's 911 call, and the cardiologist who was on call when the ambulance arrived in the early morning hours was able to open the blocked arteries. When I regained consciousness in the intensive care unit, even though I was on a ventilator, I was surrounded by my loving family, and the room was filled with an overwhelming sense of the presence of God. My first thought was, "Here we go again. I've done battle before and God has never left my side. We'll simply do battle again and I'll trust Him for the outcome, whatever it is."

Through God's abundant blessing, I have had a marvelous quality of life in between occurrences of the leukemia and following the heart attack. Since retiring from the presidency of

Oklahoma Baptist University in 1998, I have been able to remain active in teaching at Union University and in consulting with colleges, universities, private academies, churches, and other non-profit organizations. From 1998 until 2007, I served as executive director of the International Association of Baptist Colleges and Universities, supporting the work of fifty-four Baptist universities and representing them in Washington as a member of the Secretariat. I live with the haunting reality that the leukemia will return every few years, but the oncologists are very diligent at monitoring the disease. Through regular blood tests and planned visits to M.D. Anderson, we discover it early and can make preparations for whatever treatment is called for. Medical science continues to do research and find improved ways to treat both the chronic and the more acute forms of leukemia and lymphomas. For their diligence and dedication, I am deeply grateful.

Lessons I Learned

The lessons learned from five bouts with leukemia and a major heart attack are far too numerous to recount in a single chapter or even a single book, but as I have dealt with life-threatening illness for more than twenty years, I have reached some conclusions that could be helpful to others.

Never underestimate the importance of family and friends. It was such a blessing that I did not have to deal with the tough times alone. With each round of chemotherapy, my wife and daughters went through their own period of agony. Their prayers, their encouragement, and their proactive approach to searching for things that would be helpful to me stirred in me new courage to deal with each occurrence as a "player" and not a "victim." Friends beyond number took the time to call or write each time the news went out that I was dealing with the leukemia again. There is probably no blessing, beyond the blessing of the grace and presence of God, quite like the blessing of family and friends.

Do not assume that your doctors know all they need to know. We tend to assign to doctors the status of omniscience, and that is not fair to you or the doctor. When one of the leading oncologists in Oklahoma City did not know about the most current research and the possibilities that were emerging from successful tests done with an experimental drug and did not know that a leukemia patient should not receive medication that caused internal bleeding, I realized that I should not assume that doctors know all they need to know. One of the great blessings has been the doctor to whom I was referred in 1990 at M.D. Anderson, who continues to be my doctor and is so diligent and caring that I feel completely confident in her judgment and recommendations. She does not mind my questions or my efforts at interpreting blood tests, and has been most encouraging in helping me through my feelings.

Be informed. I suppose it is my nature, but I wanted to know all I could about this disease that I had never heard of; I thought leukemia was leukemia. As I became a student of the illness, I learned that there are several chronic forms of leukemia and several acute forms. I searched every source I could find to learn all I could about "hairy cell leukemia." I also realized that some doctors do not tell you all you need to know and that you cannot absorb all the information a doctor gives you in one session. Some doctors may be uncomfortable with a patient asking questions and insisting on knowing possibilities, but it is important for patients to probe and ask so they can deal more effectively with the effects and side effects of their illnesses and the treatments. Determine to be as knowledgeable as possible about your body and about the disease with which you are dealing.

Remember that prayer is the key to emotional and physical stability. Early in my spiritual pilgrimage, I became convinced that one of the most important disciplines I could develop was the discipline of daily conversation with God. There were times over the years when I felt an unusual sense of his presence as I dealt with victories, blessings, threats, and occasional bad times. I was so grateful that when I needed him, I did not have to wait for him and that prayer was not a new thing for me. As the disease increasingly limited my physical ability to go about my normal routine, I rediscovered the joy of becoming a student of prayer. For example, my awareness of prayer recognized that prayer should be persistent, seriously personal, totally honest and open, and that when I prayed, there was no time for religious games. I could express my fears, talk about my pain and discomfort, plead for help, intercede for my family and their anxiety, and praise God for his presence. My experience with a personal God who cares and to whom I matter made each occurrence a time of spiritual renewal.

Be determined to fight. A fighting spirit stands a better chance of surviving a life-threatening disease than does fatalistic resignation to the worst-case scenario. You owe it to yourself and to your family to do battle with the illness. I had never thought about the threat of dying young until the leukemia showed up. Not really knowing how long I might live or what the process of deterioration and dying would be like, I began to ask God for courage and dignity as I faced each phase and occurrence. I have been around a lot of people in their "dying days" and those who faced dying with courage and grace were such a witness to me. I wanted to be that kind of witness to my family and friends and still do.

Work on maintaining a positive, upbeat spirit. I am convinced that we can think and talk ourselves into feeling worse and being miserable. I have been around people who have done just that, and I certainly did not want people to remember me in that way. As I grappled with my weakness and deterioration in those first months, I tried hard to emphasize the positive in my conversations. I tried to talk more about hope than about the gloomy possibilities of what was happening. I tried to smile and laugh more than I frowned or groaned. I realized that my negative spirit and my gloomy conversation could actually cause me to feel worse while a positive spirit and the effort to smile and laugh could help me feel better.

Stay active. Because the fever lasted so long and my weakness and physical deterioration began to limit what I could do, one of my greatest fears was that I would lose the ability to think, learn, or reason. I had read somewhere that high fever over a sustained period could affect the brain cells, and that frightened me. I had invested so much time and effort in getting a good education, so the thought that what I had learned might be wiped away was scary. I began to look for things to do. Even though my concentration was affected by the fever and the medication, I made myself read both fiction and professional books. I looked for things I could do with my hands, light manual labor that would allow me the satisfaction of knowing that I was doing something productive. During the times when I have had to deal with a period of weakness and loss of stamina, I have been able to learn a lot about how to use the computer. Being able to research and write during those times have been therapeutic. While it may be questionable to some family members or friends that I did not suffer damage to brain cells, I think I was able to retain some functionality even in the worst times.

Exercise. Having been active, interested in, and involved in sports all my life, I was greatly bothered to see my muscles disappear and my skin turn paler than I could have imagined. I still remember the day when I glanced in the mirror as I walked by the dresser in our bedroom and noticed how frail I looked and that I was shuffling rather than walking. The shock of that sight gave me a new determination to find ways to exercise and keep up as much strength as possible. I found exercises that I could do, even in bed, like leg lifts, knee bends, use of light dumbbells, and simply flexing my arms, legs, and hips. A physical therapist recommended the use of a stationary bicycle as a way to begin to rebuild muscle tone in my legs, arms, shoulders, and back. I really think the effort to regain strength and stamina helped in the recovery process. Whether or not it did, the exercise nevertheless made me feel stronger and better able to handle the difficult times.

Conclusion

I had an elderly friend who had faced all sorts of physical problems but had maintained a positive, upbeat spirit. One day I asked her what her secret was. She replied: "I decided that when the body began to deteriorate, it was time for the spirit to begin to grow." Another elderly widow who faced life-threatening illness told me: "If the treatment doesn't work, I get to go home to be with Eddie (her husband). If the treatment works, I get to go to some more OBU basketball games. So, either way, I win." What great insight into the way to deal with life-threatening illness or circumstances. The wonderful truth for a child of God is that God is able, and more than sufficient, to supply our every need. And, either way, we win.

Befriending Fear

Kathryn Muller Lopez
Associate Professor of Religion
Department of Religion and Philosophy
Campbell University

It was dinnertime on a Wednesday night in early November 2009, and I was lying down in the bedroom. I had had surgery the week before to remove a tumor from my colon and was still feeling weak. All the biopsies before the surgery had come back negative, and the surgery had been successful; I was hoping for a speedy recovery. About five-thirty that night, the phone rang and my thirteen-year-old daughter answered it. It was the doctor. Since doctors rarely call a patient at home, much less at dinnertime, both of us were a bit taken aback. The doctor informed me that the pathology reports had come back and they had found cancer. I immediately whispered to my daughter who was still standing in the doorway, worry written all over her: "Go get your daddy." She hesitated. "Go get your daddy, now." She ran from the room.

Clearly she had communicated her worry to her father because he came running into the house. Lying on the bed, we held the phone between us listening to the doctor. I felt nothing, but I watched horror appear on my husband's face. The doctor ended by saying that he would arrange for me to see the oncologist the same day I came for my surgery follow-up. When I hung up, Allen and I continued to lie on the bed, our heads together, holding hands. Neither one of us could move. A few days later, when I was finally able to look up colon cancer on the Internet, I discovered that I had stage 3 colon cancer. The tumor had broken through the wall of the colon and had spread to the lymph nodes. In September I had had a routine colonoscopy. The doctors found a tumor too large to be removed except by surgery, but the tissue samples taken during the colonoscopy were negative for cancer. In November I went to Duke University Medical Center for the surgery, which was successful, but when the tumor and surrounding tissue were biopsied, the pathologist found cancer. My life had turned around in one ten-minute phone call.

In early December I met with the oncologist. Duke is a teaching hospital, which means I never saw just one doctor. After speaking with a med student, a resident, and a visiting doctor, the oncologist confirmed what I had discovered on the Internet, and then began to outline treatment options. That conversation will be etched into my memory for all time. He put a piece of paper in front of me. It was a printout from a Web site where a doctor can actually plug in what kind of cancer a patient has, how far advanced it is, and the patient's age and come out with (1) the patient's chances of being alive in five years, and (2) the chances of having a reoccurrence of cancer in five years. It is an overwhelming experience to have a piece of paper tell you what your chances of living or dying might be.

They immediately implanted a port in the right side of my chest with a tube that flowed straight into my jugular vein, and the doctor recommended the following course of treatment: Every three weeks I would receive a drug called Oxaliplatin intravenously. The second drug, Xeloda, was available in pill form, and because the doctor said that the pill was no less effective than the intravenous form, I opted to take the pill. The plan was that I would take two pills in the morning and three at night, beginning on the same day I received the Oxaliplatin, and continuing for two weeks. I would then have one week off before starting again, with six months of treatment overall. The doctor asked if I would like to wait until after Christmas, but

Allen and I looked at each other and simultaneously said no. I would begin as soon as they could get me an appointment. My mother-in-law was coming to help for Christmas, and there seemed to be no compelling reason to wait.

Over the next few days as I prepared for chemo, I began to realize that my life would never be the same. Illnesses had always seemed to me like bad houseguests: They were a pain to have around, but you knew that the time would come when they would leave. Not so with cancer. There is no way to know when it will leave, or what state it will leave you in when it does. And there is always the fear that it won't ever leave. Cancer comes and your life is changed forever.

Back home, my church family and friends began to organize and mobilize. What kind of help did I need and when? They also began a campaign of encouragement. For instance, while I was in the hospital on heavy painkillers, I spent a day hallucinating penguins marching in formation around the walls of my hospital room. Later, I remembered hearing about the use of visualization in cancer treatment, and it occurred to me that, like *March of the Penguins*, my visualization would be imagining mother penguins carrying the drugs to any spot where there might be cancer and, braving all odds, feeding the chemo straight to the cancer cells. The daddy penguins would remain behind to protect my healthy lymph nodes. I went out and got a stuffed penguin as a mascot. I named him "Semi-colon" because a student had jokingly asked me that since I had had some of my "colon" removed, did I now have a "semi-colon"? Then a friend gave me another penguin, and we called him "Node," as in "lymph node." He represented the strength in my body to fight off the cancer. Then the avalanche started: I now have a major collection of penguin-related items!

Receiving chemo is like entering a parallel reality. It began when I received the Xeloda in the mail. It came in an innocent-looking brown envelope marked as medical supplies. Inside was a bottle of pills neatly bubble wrapped. When I unrolled the bottle, I momentarily freaked out: It was labeled with the warnings "Biohazard," and "Do not handle without gloves," and other really scary stuff. I actually wondered to myself if I should find some latex gloves in order to take the medicine. When I said this out loud to my husband, he just looked at me. What did it matter if I touched it, I was going to swallow it! As pointless as it was, I could never bring myself to touch the pills. I would shake them out on a paper towel and drop them straight into my mouth.

I started Xeloda the same day I received the Oxaliplatin. Intravenous chemotherapy takes place in a cancer center— basically a big room full of reclining chairs. There are no walls, and the curtains are almost never pulled. The nurses want to be able to see you at any given moment from any place in the room. Chemo has a very set routine. For me, they began by accessing the port and taking blood, which got sent over to the lab for testing. It could take up to an hour to get the results back, at which point the doctor could see if I was healthy enough to receive chemo, or if there were any other problems indicated by the blood tests. Before I received the Oxaliplatin, the nurses gave me a dose of steroids and antihistamines in order to cut down on the chance of rejection. About two hours later, when the Oxaliplatin was done, they flushed the port with a blood thinner to stop clotting, removed the IV, and sent me home. I could not have faced this time alone, nor did I have to. I truly thank those who had the strength to sit with me during those long hours.

And so the treatment began. I had taken off the end of the fall semester because of the surgery, and now I had to figure out what would happen while I was receiving chemo. In the end, I was given the opportunity to teach part-time rather than full-time. It might be a bit extreme to say that this saved me, but it made a huge difference in my ability to get better. If I had sat on my sofa alone for six months, I would have become so depressed that my body would have been weakened by the state of my spirit. I needed to feel like I was doing something productive. On the other hand, teaching part-time gave me the chance to get the rest I needed to keep my strength and still feel connected with my world.

So what does chemotherapy do to a person? The drugs I was on did not generally cause hair loss or nausea. The most intense side effect was sensitivity to cold. I remember needing to wear long underwear, extra layers of pants, shirts, and socks. Indoors or out, I was rarely without a hat and a scarf. At home I used blankets, set the heater high, kept the gas fireplace going, and sometimes used a space heater. The only difference between inside and out was that outside I wore a heavy coat. I could not inhale, eat, or drink anything that was cooler than my body temperature without suffering severe jaw pain or the sensation that my mouth and throat were closing up.

Then came a relentless fatigue that got progressively worse over the six months of treatment, and lingers even to today. There were days it seemed I slept more than I was awake. One morning I looked in the mirror and realized that the bags under my eyes had bags of their own. All I could think was thank goodness for glasses—at least they hid some of my face. Muscle weakness is another part of chemo, and between that and the fatigue, I was almost helpless at times. For instance, I could barely close the back of my minivan. I still carry an image of myself hanging from the strap on the back door of my van like a small child, feet dangling in the air in an attempt to put all my weight into it, too weak to close it by myself.

Along with the fatigue and muscle weakness came "chemo brain": a serious decrease in my ability to focus. I was easily confused. I had a hard time following through on an idea, I would forget what I was saying in the middle of a sentence, and I could not read more than a few pages of a book before forgetting what I'd just read. This was a huge loss of self. I make my living by thinking, reading, and teaching. It's a little like an athlete losing his or her coordination. Who was I without this?

Soon after the treatment began, the skin on my feet started to peel off, like a chemical burn from the inside. Red spots began to appear on and around my nose. I felt like Rudolph the Red Nose Reindeer; it seemed so unfair! After a few months of treatment, I also developed neuropathy, nerve damage in my fingers and toes. I did not finish all the doses of the Oxaliplatin because the doctor was afraid the damage would become permanent. My toes are still affected. While not bad, the neuropathy is the daily reminder of the war I fought.

Besides the side effects, there are all the little emergencies that come along with chemo. First there were the emergency room visits. Sometimes a trip to the hospital helped a lot. There were a lot of good doctors out there, but sometimes they did not help much. I found that sometimes just an IV bag of saline made a world of difference because at least I went home hydrated. But there were times that left me frustrated and bewildered. One time I went to the emergency room because I was cramping very badly and was quickly becoming dehydrated. The entire experience was awful and full of indignities both big and small. For example, it's very difficult to give a urine sample while connected to an IV. Those things are on wheels, but, still, awkward does not even begin to describe it. And finally, when the doctor came in to give me the results of all the tests, he told me that I had the flu, and he gave me a prescription for nausea. My husband and I were speechless. I was not nauseated in the least. I had colon cancer and I was suffering from severe diarrhea. I'm not a medical doctor, but really? The flu?

During my second "favorite" trip to the emergency room, the nurse ended up coming into the room saying, "The good news is that your blood tests came back normal; the bad news is that we don't know what's wrong with you. I'm going to go get the discharge papers so you can go home." I started to cry. I was sick, and I was terrified by what was happening to me. The nurse left when the tears started and back in walked the physician's assistant who, with a hearty smile on her face, said, "I hear you're upset. Why are you crying?" Even today, I can't think of that encounter without bewilderment and hurt. Who would not be crying or at least wanting to cry? I came to the hospital for answers. Is it not reasonable to expect some help, however minimal? Is it not reasonable to be upset when told to go home without an answer and be just as sick as when you came in?

The chemo finally ended in June, but it left me severely anemic. I couldn't handle taking iron tablets because my stomach was already eaten up by the chemo, and it just hurt too much. This left IV iron transfusions, which were unpleasant in their own way, but by mid-July I was free. No more treatments, just recovery. I had a wonderful summer enjoying the warmth and time with my family. I learned to kayak, which I love, and walked and walked and walked.

While all of this was going on with my body, I found myself feeling mentally detached from what was happening to me. Like being in the center of the storm, everything was spinning around me. So much of my focus was on just getting through the day that the larger picture faded into the background, and in the center of the storm there was silence and a peculiar peace. Inside that place I did a lot of thinking. I never asked the question, "Why me?" And I never felt any anger toward God. After all: Why not me? Why anyone? This is God's message to Job in Job 38–42, the voice from the whirlwind. How could I possibly understand how creation works, or fully grasp my place in it? God's words are both an admonishment and an encouragement. Having let go of the need to have everything make sense, I was able to believe truly and deeply something I had always known in my head: I am loved by God unconditionally, without any reservation, deeper than any human could love me. Even more, I came to know that God was with me every step of the way through my cancer treatments, and because of that I did not need to fear.

In the process of working through this, I do think I scared a few people. My husband later told me that one of his worst moments was the day I told him that I was not afraid to die. Now I can look back and see how terrifying that moment was for him. I think he heard me say that I was giving up, but that is not what I meant at all. What I was trying to tell him was that I was letting go of the fear. Fear is so debilitating. It is no way to live and it is definitely not a place in which to dwell when you're fighting off a potentially deadly disease. However, I don't want to leave the impression that this is easy to do, that I said, "Oh, I'm just not going to be afraid anymore," as if a person can turn fear on or off like a light switch. No, for me the letting go of fear came because I learned that it is fear, including the fear of dying, that stops us from living. Lyrics like "live like you're dying" or "if today were your last day" never resonated with me. We are all dying whether we want to think about it or not. What I learned was that my goal as a Christian is to live, and fear only gets in the way.

As I worked to find peace, I found walking to be very therapeutic. I listened to my iPod, to requiems in particular, the Latin mass for the dead. People looked at me kind of funny when I told them this, but the words, as far as I knew them, were so comforting, and the music sank deep into my soul:

Requiem æternam dona eis, Domine,
et lux perpetua luceat eis.

Eternal rest grant unto them, O Lord,
and let perpetual light shine upon them.

Et lux perpetua: Perpetual light. This phrase just kept going around and around in my head. I had been so cold, living in a dark place for what seemed like forever. Through the music I would ease into the place of light and let my soul rest there. Living or dying, we are all surrounded by perpetual light.

I got most of my energy back during the summer following treatment and was ready to return to a full schedule of activities in the fall, healthy and capable. The one-year anniversary of when they discovered the tumor was 23 September 2010. Anniversaries can be tough, and that was true for me. Having cancer had taken over my life to such an extent that I was stunned by the reminder of all that had taken place in the span of a single year. Moreover, the one-year anniversary also marked the next phase in my life with cancer, the testing to see if I still had cancer or not. I had a couple of scans and another colonoscopy, and by the middle of October I found out that I was completely cancer-free. The treatment had worked. I will have to meet with the oncologist on a regular basis for the next few years, but right now I am free and I refuse to live in fear of what may happen down the road.

After the news got out about my good report, a friend asked me what it felt like to be a miracle. I was pretty thoroughly blown away by this statement. I am not a miracle. My healing was caused by the doctors, my treatment, my mental state, people's prayers, their acts of kindness and concern, as well as by their surprises of small gifts, funny cards, and food. There's nothing miraculous about what happened to me, except for the fact that so many people showed the love of Christ to me by loving me through this. But maybe that's the answer. If Jesus' ability to perform miracles was a sign of God's presence with him, then maybe I am a miracle and my community is the miracle maker. God was present with everyone who showed me love, who prayed for me, who sat with me when I needed help, who watched my kids when I could not, who helped my husband deal with his fears. I am a miracle because I am the visible sign of God's presence with us, the Christian community, my church, and my family and friends spread throughout the country. Thank all of you, wherever you are, for being God's presence to me, who prayed for and helped me. You are the miracle makers. And for everyone who reads this book, when you pray, offer a word of comfort, bring a meal, or whatever you may do in the name of Christ for someone walking the journey through cancer, you, too, are a miracle maker.

One of the Better Cancers to Get

C. Douglas Weaver
Associate Professor of Religion
Director of Undergraduate Studies
Department of Religion
Baylor University

In June 2011, my mother had surgery for a broken hip, so I spent several days on the fifth floor of the hospital. One day, I ventured to the fourth floor and walked down the hall to the place where my father had died of colon cancer in 1983. I had driven by this hospital many times during visits to see my mother and had looked up at the room, which is visible from a main thoroughfare. But that hot June day was the first time that I had been inside the hospital since 1983.

Watching my father die of cancer was a traumatic experience. The debilitating pain and suffering of cancer—well, it was no easy death. Dying peacefully while asleep was not the image seared into my soul as I witnessed the last moments of his life. Cancer really was the C word—a curse word. Of course, no one likes the word, but I came to despise and fear it.

I was a doctoral student in seminary at the time and felt compelled to theologize in a diary about my dad's last days. For several years afterward, I preached about events surrounding his cancer and death to many churches in which I served as interim pastor.

The loss of my father had a profound effect on many people, including my wife, Pat; she had entered seminary under my father's ministerial tutelage. My son, Aaron, born three months before Dad's death, lost what I knew would be the best "grandy" on the face of the earth.

Unbelievably, the following year my mother was also diagnosed with colon cancer. In her case, the surgery was successful. Her cancer was caught very early; she was cured and never had any more problems with cancer.

Thankfully, no one spoke the phrase to me that one of my seminary professors had used to handle his own journey with family tragedy: "the Lord giveth and the Lord taketh away." That kind of thinking did not work for me. While I was obviously ecstatic that my mother was fine, I found no relief while grappling with the ugliness of cancer and death.

Throughout the journey of grief, I never really made much sense of "why bad things happen to good people," even though I read numerous books on the subject. I never denied that God worked good out of bad circumstances, but cancer was really bad, and I did not see any good. When people said that hearing of my father's death brought them back to the faith, I thought to myself that surely God could have used other methods to do that.

Eventually, I latched onto the phrase "dysteleological suffering" to describe the senseless suffering that accompanies cancer and many other tragedies. I also held more intensely the belief that Jesus suffered for us and with us on the cross. Always searching theologically, one thing was clear: I did not see any intentional will of God in senseless suffering. My theology was forever rooted in this experience of the C word—and I never found any glory in any form of cancerous predestined providence.

For two decades after my father's death, I had the pleasure of frequent colonoscopies. "You are the son of two parents with colon cancer—it is not if, but when, you get it yourself"—was the message of one doctor to my brother. In the early years, I did a great job changing my diet to very healthy menu items before apostasizing: Those dastardly whole wheat noodles ruined any pleasure I had in eating.

Colon cancer never came—and I am very grateful for that—but the C word did come to me.

I was diagnosed with bladder cancer in 2006. I learned that it is a disease often associated with smokers—so much for having never let one cigarette touch my lips. I also found out that "if you have cancer, bladder cancer is one of the better ones to get." Cheery thought, that. "Yours is on the surface of the bladder," my doctor explained. "People hardly ever die from this." That was indeed great news. Some of my best friends, nevertheless, urged me to be aggressive in my treatment since information from reputable online sources noted that some people did die from bladder cancer.

Who knows whether the terrible bout with kidney stones I had in 2000 was a precursor to future pain with my urological equipment. I guess not. But my kidney stones did at least expose me to the folks at an urologist's office, and later I decided that those stones were symbolic of the fundamentalist stone throwing I experienced at the small Baptist college in Georgia, where I taught.

In 2003, I joined the faculty of Baylor University's Department of Religion, and the C word began to reveal itself to me in a religious atmosphere—Texas high school football. My daughter, Andrea, made the high school cheerleading squad, and Friday night lights became our weekend entertainment. One fall night in 2005, I simply could not sit still in the stands. I felt piercing pain—it was like a knife in the penis, which is what I began to constantly tell my urologist.

The shooting pains would come and go, and I developed a strong sting whenever I voided. Urine tests were negative. The doctor performed multiple cystoscopes. During the first one, I just about went through the roof as he tried to maneuver the expensive camera around my prostate. He halted the procedure. I am certain that he and his nurse—both skilled professionals—thought I was crazy or acting like a baby. Clearly, I was going to be the topic of conversation in doctors' and nurses' lounges as they discussed this new patient's amazingly low tolerance for pain. Low tolerance, high tolerance, it was a moot point: I felt the pressure and the piercing knife pains—I was not making it up. Valium was ordered for subsequent procedures with hopes that it would relax all or parts of my body. It did not help much, especially the time that a substitute nurse forgot to use the numbing gel. Eventually my body, or the nurses' skill, won the day, and I was less of a pain.

As the bladder pain persisted throughout 2005, the doctor gave me several different medicines for "pee pain." They never relieved the pain, but they made the urine turn colors. Sometimes, I was the Red Sea. Sometimes, I was burnt orange, which, according to my doctor, was great for Texas Longhorn fans. I reminded him that I taught at Baylor, but he had no green and gold. Using these meds meant that I should have always used the public toilet with a door, but habits are hard to break. I often went hurrying to the open line of urinals. I did feel sorry for those gentlemen who had the misfortune of using these public facilities after me since the water pressure in urinals is not what it used to be in the old days. It was a colorful experience for all.

For a year, I battled urinary discomfort but had little or no success with the colorful meds. I stopped drinking caffeine (ultimately for two years) since the doctor said it grabbed and squeezed the bladder. Sitz baths were recommended for relaxation. I can sit in pretty hot water, but such fiery hydrotherapy proved useless for me except for making me look discolored all over. My doctor referred to me as a "cerebral gentleman" since I was a professor, and, for a while, he

32

appeared to be looking for answers in my head rather than in other parts of my anatomy. Well, maybe not all in my head. He once referenced the latest studies from India, which noted that frequent sex sometimes helped with those suffering from bladder problems. Simply put, Nirvana surely was not the answer.

I did not blame the doctor for being cautious about the severity of my case. My "knife in the penis" explanation was a bit graphic, but my test results, including exploratory biopsies, kept turning up negative. A year passed, and I had no relief from pain. Going to the bathroom was getting more difficult. I experienced terrible urges, ran to the commode, had muscle spasms, but voided little and always at the speed of a trickle. Once when this happened at a movie theater, I bent over in pain and half-cried to my son, "I know there is something wrong with me."

And there was. After another biopsy, the doctor said, "Your bladder is really red." Given the number of tests I had already had, he said it might be a "deep tissue infection." It was not. Lab results indicated bladder cancer (on the surface, not invasive).

Of course, I began to read and hear about how treatable the cancer was. However, hearing the C word brought back memories of my father. I had to fight the fear. Friends said I should go to the M.D. Anderson Cancer Center, the world-renowned cancer center that was only three hours away in Houston. However, I liked my doctor and did not want to delay my treatment. Everything we read and everyone we talked to said the same thing. The one "gold star standard" treatment for this cancer is BCG, a chemical wash of the bladder that is done once a week for six weeks. An attenuated form of tuberculosis is injected into the bladder via a tube inserted into the penis—another of the wonders of modern medicine.

Over the course of the six weeks, I did pretty well. After each treatment, side effects usually included fever and flu-like feelings for a day. I also experienced an intense burning for several hours when voiding the chemical from my body. For some treatments the burning was a manageable fire; other times it felt like gehenna. After a day or two, the burning subsided but the sting never really went away. I also began to sweat profusely during the night. I would wear up to four shirts a night, drenching my clothes and the bed sheets on a regular basis. (Note: the sweating never stopped and still occurs six years later, especially during subsequent treatment phases. I have visited two infectious disease physicians to make sure that the BCG did not give me a bit of TB).

As the treatments wore on, I experienced fatigue. However, I never missed work, and I even went on a professional trip. Because of a hotel room mix-up, I shared a room one night with a colleague from another university. I failed to tell him about the colorful urine, and he bolted out of the bathroom asking if I was contagious. After I assured him that the parting of the Red Sea was a miracle and not a plague, he became the compassionate academic once again.

Easily the most adventurous side effect of BCG treatments was a loss of bladder control, a phenomenon not experienced by most people on a BCG regimen (but I have not really asked around much either). It did not happen initially, but would soon become a common staple whenever I had treatments. There were times when I could have been a walking advertisement for Depends disposable undergarments; they really worked. But there were also times when I could have sued the manufacturer; they failed me miserably. Of course, there was no way to know when I would experience loss of control, so I wore dark pants to work almost every day while I was being treated. I worried about classroom performance since I am not one to stand behind a podium to teach. The podium, however, was a necessary cover a few times.

At work, I have a nice office, but it is not close to a restroom. Folks often saw me walking fast in the hall or trotting in the chapel (a holy run) to avoid failure. At times, I successfully held the urge, but usually my face turned flush red as the knife piercing sensation dug deep, and I would bend over in pain. The worst times for me occurred when people whom I did not know were in my office, including prospective students and their families. During those visits, getting to the restroom was impossible. It was a helpless feeling. Office guests hopefully never knew what was going on.

I remember one day, though, when I forgot to wear my dark pants. My khakis got drenched. I had a folder that held materials explaining the religion major to students, and I kept it safely in my hand hiding the deluge. All was well until a family got up to leave. I reached out to shake their hands and handed them the folder, which they needed. Immediately, I knew that I was uncovered and felt like the time I was six years old, hearing my first grade teacher calling my mother with the request to bring more clothes to school. Put more biblically, I wondered why Amos ever thought an ever-flowing stream was a good picture of justice. Of course, I laughed about it later, but the embarrassment that the C word could inflict sometimes played on my psyche when I was dependent upon un-dependable Depends.

After my cancer treatments were completed, I waited anxiously to see if the BCG worked. When I got the call from the doctor, I was in my office and my graduate assistant was there. She smiled as I cried a few tears of joy.

Because bladder cancer has a high rate of return, the protocol is for patients to have "maintenance therapy" (love those medical euphemisms), which included three BCG treatments every six months for three years or so, depending on whether a person's body can tolerate the BCG. My body could not. After only two treatments in the spring 2007, I developed an infection, fever, and pain so severe that using the bathroom was beyond dreadful. The doctor stopped the treatments but said that I would still be monitored closely with a cystoscope every three months.

All was well until June 2008, when I attended the annual meeting of the Cooperative Baptist Fellowship and fell off the wagon, drinking a ton of Coca Cola on Beale Street in Memphis (yes, it was Coke; meet a real teetotaler). When I returned home, I had a bladder pain flare-up, but the pain soon went away, and caffeine was the suggested culprit. I wondered if this occurrence was a sign to come—and it was. I began having atypical urine cultures (not negative, but not positive for cancer cells either). The doctor reaffirmed that he was watching closely and that the atypicals were possible for persons whose bladders had been battered by BCG treatments. That made good medical sense, but the "pee sting" had returned, and my mind played doctor. The first time it had taken a while for the cancer to show. Was the pattern repeating itself?

I will never forget where I was when I heard the C word again. In April 2009, I was in Indianapolis, Indiana, to give addresses to the North Central region of the Cooperative Baptist Fellowship. I had just arrived at the hotel when my cell phone rang. Sitting in a car with a very nice person (someone I had never met before), my doctor told me that the bladder cancer had returned but that the tests results indicated that the kidney was involved this time, too. More than a bit stunned, I exited the car, knowing that I was to speak in just a few hours. My mind raced, but the speaking engagement helped me to focus on something else for a while.

With the news about the kidney, my doctor sent me to see a specialist in Dallas. He questioned whether the cancer was in the kidney and suggested it was contaminated results "bleeding over" from the bladder. He added that trying to throw the BCG into the kidney via a stent—a method some doctors used—was a poor option ("no research data that indicates it works"). He also pushed me to attack the cancer in the bladder again since there was no question that it had returned there. With optimistic bluntness, he concluded, "I think we can fix that bladder and hopefully you can keep it for up to five more years. If not, you will be a BCG failure, and you will need to discuss the next step: removing the bladder and having a reconstructed one made."

Needless to say, on the drive home to Waco with my wife, I had mixed emotions. I hoped the specialist was correct about the kidney (he would be), but I was anxious. The message that even if the BCG worked this time, my bladder had limited time in my body was an unwanted wakeup call.

During the summer of 2009, I received six more BCG treatments—at a reduced dosage—because of my prior strong reactions to the medicine. I was anxious about a reduced dosage working, but it did. All of the side effects of the first round were there—and even more pronounced. My body was taking the BCG but was not happy about it.

Then came the summer of 2009. When the C word rained, it poured. As I began my treatments, Pat was diagnosed with uterine cancer. She immediately had surgery, which was successful. Soon after I completed my treatments, she began an extensive round of radiation. She is now fine.

With my two bouts of bladder cancer behind me, the doctor recommended that I try the "maintenance therapy" again. Every six months of 2010 and 2011, I received the beloved BCG. Each time the dosage was reduced because of my reaction (reaction was good, the doctor assured me, but my reactions were just too "good"). In the spring 2011, the last treatment cycle was completed. It would have been hard to go below the final dosage I received: 1/100 of the original prescription.

As I reflect on and share my experiences, I am grateful that "if you have cancer, this is one of the better ones to get." I have never thought about what I had to deal with in comparison to what my father (and many, many others) have gone through. At the same time, I do recognize and affirm that the C word comes in all shapes and sizes and that I wish I had not gotten it in any form.

A hot topic today is the interaction between the individual and the community in the Christian faith. Some now only focus on community, citing the excessive individualism of our past. My experience with cancer highlights for me (beyond the ivory tower of academics where the conversation rages) that faith is both/and. Cancer has been my individual, personal pain (no one could wear the Depends for me). When I lay in bed thinking that my cancer involved my bladder and my kidney, I never stopped knowing that Jesus was with me. I did find assurance from my wife's constant comfort. But in the end, mine was an intensely personal fear, lying in the darkness wondering what was happening to me. Theology is never simply what a group of people talk about; it is a lived experience. My cancer and living with the effects of my father's cancer are interpretive lenses for my life and faith. Individual laments are in the Bible, I believe.

Throughout this cancer journey, I have, of course, needed the Christian community. The folks in Lott, Texas, where I served as an interim pastor when I was first diagnosed, were gracious beyond measure. I have written this chapter intentionally without names so as not to miss the names of those who have walked with me. In addition to my family, I have had many friends who made this journey with me. They know who they are, and I have inflicted "TMI" (too much information) upon many of them. The ministry of Christ's church is our hope and promise.

I have often approached the anxiety of the cancer with humor—that is obvious, I am sure, in my writing—but lest readers think I have always handled this journey with spiritual aplomb, my friends know better. In fact, sin sat crouching at the door and often pounced. For with a judgmental spirit, I found myself wondering why some folks who made such a big deal about community and spirituality never reached out to me when there was opportunity.

My wonderfully hectic job at Baylor University and my beautiful family usually allow me to push excessive anxiety about the C word to the back of the brain. During my first episode of cancer, I was on tenure track in a publish/perish environment, and that no doubt gave my mind other things to think about. Yet, the anxiety-producing reality that bladder cancer often returns never disappears. Perhaps it is telling that I—as an educator—have refused to educate myself fully on what it means to have bladder removal surgery or to have a reconstructed bladder installed.

I hope that day is not soon. But in late June 2011, test results came back from my latest urine culture: a positive. Another test is scheduled in July. If it is positive, a biopsy will follow. Do I think this will be a third episode of cancer? Yes. Do I pray that my latest result is a false positive? Of course. Will I have a new bladder by the time this book is published? E-mail me to see! With hope and yes, anxiety.

Objects in Mirror Are Closer Than They Appear

Paula B. Hooper
Retired Staff Member and
Current Active Member
First Baptist Church, Athens, Georgia

I am a big fan of mirrors. One autumn, when I rearranged my office at First Baptist Church in Athens, Georgia, where I was serving as administrative assistant, I made certain that among bookshelves and framed artwork, a mirror would land on a tucked-away wall adjacent to my desk. I openly confess to being prissy, especially on Wednesdays when the conclusion of my work day would parlay into family night supper, choir for four-year-olds, and adult choir rehearsal. You better believe I stole more than one glance in my looking glass on those days. An entire Estée Lauder makeup job could be wiped out in forty-five minutes by a room full of four-year-olds who would rather lasso each other with hula hoops than sing "Jesus Loves Me."

So on the day I received a phone call at work from my physician to drop everything I was doing, call my husband, and come to his office pronto, what did I do first? What any normal person would, of course: I primped in my mirror. The seemingly healthy visage looking back at me confirmed that some horrific mistake had been made. I could not possibly be so sick as to warrant an emergency trip to the doctor's office. "Once I arrive, this mix-up will be straightened out," I thought. "I'll be back to finish the newsletter in no time."

My newsletter remained unfinished that day.

Instead of returning to the routine tasks on my desk, I began an entirely new journey as my physician, in his quiet and compassionate manner, presented me with a diagnosis of cancer.

Two weeks shy of my fiftieth birthday and this was what I got. Everything in that sixty-second span of bad news became a strange dichotomy in time; it raced in an uncomprehendingly rapid blur while simultaneously slugging past me like a slow-motion movie. I will always think it strange that before I could absorb what the doctor was actually saying to me, my attention was drawn to the most unconnected things: the droning sound of the fluorescent lighting (what pitch is that, anyway?); the way my husband's hands were folded and the crisp cuff of his suit pants; and the doleful color of endless floor tiles that have apparently covered fields of medical building floors since Hippocrates.

Then, voilà: Just like that, I had cancer. It was almost akin to hearing someone say, "Mrs. Hooper, you need a crown on that lower left molar." The office personnel assumed their individual roles, and the next thing I knew clipboards came out of nowhere, serving as dance floors for rapidly tapping pens, scheduling visits with oncologists, surgeons, and radiologists. Medical terminology that I relegated to people on Wednesday night prayer lists now came flying at me like angry bees.

"Insurance card, Mrs. Hooper? Could you fill out this form? Ever had an MRI? Who's your primary care doctor? Got your calendar? What's your husband's cell number? Is your daughter Amanda? You signed this in the wrong place. Don't lose this; don't misplace that. For this test you just go down that hallway past two doors, take a left...." I felt frozen as I watched my husband, Charlie, jump up and run interference for me without missing a beat.

Unbeknownst to me, this was the day I would begin my slow realization that the objects in my mirror were closer than they appeared.

Socrates once said, "The unexamined life is not worth living." Though the Greek philosopher's statement may seem ill fitting in this story, I assure you that it is not. It turned out to be pivotal in my life. Ironically, even though I was an English teacher in years past, I have never been particularly moved by the wisdom of Socrates, nor of any other Greek philosopher. That changed for me, however, when this maxim took root in my life. Had I not been navigating such an unwelcome valley, I would have never understood its significance. My mirror was about to become the subject of much deeper examination than a superficial glance to see if I had lipstick on my teeth. It was about to become a conduit that would bring me to the sobering task of facing myself in a new light, examining myself far beyond the physical level.

The first thing I had to face in my mirror was not only the acceptance of cancer, but also the sobering reality of the little girl in me who was ill-equipped to handle the arduous journey that lay ahead. Admitting that I had a lot of maturing to do was a difficult truth to face.

Accepting abrupt change in life does not happen instantly, and I learned that I had to get out of my comfort zone and be a responsible player in my own treatment and healing. Being proactive is difficult for me, as I tend to be reticent, trusting those around me, and leaving the difficult decisions in the hands of someone whom I deem more qualified than I. Thus began my initial growth phase as I jumped into the driver's seat against my will.

No one could give me a day off from cancer; I could receive encouragement, strength, and endurance from others, but the journey was mine. Shedding my tendency to look to others to magically fix what I could not, I began making myself think through decisions more intentionally, analyzing my options, and asking questions along the way. In my possession was usually an ongoing, handwritten list of questions I had for the doctors or assistants at every office visit, and on more than one occasion I would call the office to solicit the answers I needed. I practiced anticipatory thinking, as my daughter calls it, on a daily basis where I had to make myself observe, connect dots, and stay two steps ahead. Though this mode of thinking is easy for so many, it was a huge learning curve for me. A great faith lesson I learned was that God is our strength when we bless ourselves enough to cut our own apron strings and grow up.

A second truth I learned during this time was the need for a periodic check of my personal value system. A diagnosis of cancer will do that to you in a jiffy. When was the last time I really examined the things I valued, or assessed what meant the most to me? Surely the list was more substantive at fifty than it had been at thirty. I found myself once again on a steep learning curve in which one who valued mirrors was about to see another object that was much closer than it appeared.

My doctors determined that I had squamous cell carcinoma. In my mind, its very name conjured up images of black cauldrons. This type of cancer, though not rare, is seen much less frequently than many other cancers. The regimen for treating it was difficult and laborious. But for a prissy like me, the worst thing about my cancer was its location. If I had to have cancer, why couldn't it be on my elbow, or my third toe, or the back of my knee? Instead, mine had to be cancer of the derriere.

"Oh, where is your cancer," others would inquire. "Ummm, my colon," I would respond. "Oh, my. How much of your colon was removed? Was it toward the stomach area?" they would persist. "No," I would drone in monotone, hoping the great inquisition would stop here.

Undaunted, my questioners would trudge onward. "Well, my uncle Fred had twelve inches of his colon out (poor thing, God rest his soul), and so did that deacon in our church who complains about the elevator all the time. Was it like their surgery?"

I am in torture. Finally, when I feel my booty is backed as far as it can go into a very deep corner, I run my white flag up the pole and surrender, "It's my derriere!" relieved that I've finally put it out on the airwaves.

As time passed, I actually became quite adept at shelving my vanity while still maintaining some element of decorum. So much so that when an acquaintance asked me several weeks later, "Paula, where did you have your surgery?" I confidently blurted out, "My derriere!" Upon which he choked on his chewing gum, righted his golf cap, and said, "No, Paula," I mean "where" did you have your surgery. "Atlanta? Texas? Athens?"

"Oops." Too much learning curve, perhaps?

Dealing with my type of cancer was difficult on many levels. I, who hardly darkened the grocery store doors without donning matching shoes and toenail polish, became subject to what I considered then the most undignified of medical treatment.

Diagnosed on a Thursday, I was on the operating table the following Monday morning. The surgery alone was painful, the recovery time no better, and any shred of modesty I had went out the hospital door. Christmas flew past in a blur, and December 26 capped it off with the beginning of both my chemotherapy and radiation treatments. I began chemo through a drip pump, attached to me twenty-four hours a day for six days via a PIC line inserted in my arm. I would then be free of chemo for five weeks, at which time I would wear the pump for one more final week.

Radiation jumped right in line with surgery and chemo, erecting what seemed to me to be insurmountable hurdles. I was scheduled to have thirty treatments, delivered five days a week for seven consecutive weeks. At that time, the fourth week was relegated as a recovery week, in which no radiation was administered.

When the radiologist and technicians marked a "field" for my radiation, I felt like a topographical map of Finland. My pelvis served as the country's boundaries, anchored with permanent pinpoint markings on my hips. "I cannot get through this. That's it. Period. I cannot do this," was my only thought, winding like a ribbon through my head. I was humiliated. I've always applauded those who enter the health field, especially since both my deceased mother and my daughter chose nursing as their profession. But at this point, I really wished the technicians attending to me were all as female as Dolly Parton. But that strapping young man who so ably assisted alongside the ladies was not turning into Dolly in this lifetime.

Lying on the table that day, I recalled from my college days as an English major the literary movement in Germany known as *Sturm und Drang*. To us, "Storm and Stress." Occurring from the 1760s to 1780s, this type of literature is defined in part by extremes in emotion given to free expression. This was my own personal *Sturm und Drang*. How I wanted to express my emotions in the extreme; instead, I squelched tears and summoned visions of John Wayne riding a horse: "Be tough, Paula. You can do this."

I'm sure Socrates would agree with me that a radiation table is a fine place for self-examination. I had plenty of time, no place to go, no TV to watch, no iPod, and a complimentary barren green wall as my inspiration. Through the days that found me morphing from "Wow, Dr. Terry, this radiation isn't bad at all" (day four), to "Gee, Dr. Terry, wild horses cannot drag me to that radiation table again" (day twenty-three), I thought. I thought about how badly my derriere would hurt when I got up from that hard table. I thought about what I would do if the timer malfunctioned during radiation, and I would wind up getting forty seconds of radiation instead of twenty. Consequently, I never failed to count each second, and I fortunately never had cause to worry. I thought about my will, tucked in a fireproof file drawer.

The radiation surroundings were oppressive, and I found myself in a miasma in which negative thoughts tried to take root. So to combat this, I purposely set out to think of everything that was going right for me. Although I found this task a bit difficult at first, it didn't take long until I had created a "gratitude journal" in my head. Through creating this journal of sorts, I began to have the ability to face radiation with less dread and anxiety. I made myself appreciate some remote thing, virtue, place, or circumstance that I would normally never think about.

Radiation never became pleasant for me, and there were days when, in the management of pain, I could only conjure up enough gratitude to thank Stouffer's for making Crock Pot Chicken in a Bag. But I had something to hold on to that was positive, and it came from making myself observe the world around me, of which I had previously been oblivious.

Again, what I didn't realize was that through these hours on the radiation table the objects in my mirror were looming closer than they appeared.

As the weeks of treatment progressed, every box on my checklist became marked. Loss of appetite: check. Loss of energy and toss of cookies: check. Loss of hair: check. Tendency to whine: no check. Wait a minute. No check? I knew myself well enough to know that in my never-ending endeavor to have life organized, prioritized and sanitized, I should be whining full throttle about the wrench thrown my way. So, what's up with this? My third huge discovery was on its way.

Cancer patients will tell you that waiting rooms become almost as familiar as a den recliner. Your schedule falls in sync with other patients, whom you begin to know as fellow comrades. Starting out with a bang, I decided I could be one of the fighters I always read about. "They fought cancer valiantly,"

I would read in the magazine articles residing ubiquitously throughout every office and lab I visited. But my fighter spirit took a real hit mid-way into my treatments, and my trips to the fondly named radiation "spa" were growing intolerable. I began to grow disappointed with myself because I certainly didn't feel like a warrior, even though I was supposed to be one. But then, I felt I was supposed to do a lot of things that I didn't do during this time.

It also didn't help my quest that the waiting line for radiation was so sharply skewed. Number of patients receiving radiation for breast cancer: fifteen. Number of colon cancer patients of the derriere category: one. As several ladies assembled each day to wait in line to have their breast cancer radiation, I sat isolated on the other side of the hallway, with nary a soul coming behind me (pun intended) to receive the same radiation as I. My mind wandered back to fifth grade when the softball captain selected her team during recess. I cringed with a sweat-laden brow as she called out the names of her top picks. "Oh, please, please, pleeeeze call my name before you reach the very last one," I would quietly plead to myself. And if my name was called out with the prefix "and lastly," well I might as well have packed it up and gone home because the rest of the day I felt like an outsider looking in.

My self-pity was short-lived that day in the waiting room, for I quickly came back to reality from my fifth-grade moment of reverie, and thought about how all of us in the waiting room felt like outsiders looking in. Though a simple revelation, it was a lightning bolt zap to me when I realized how much I had learned from the nameless people I encountered each day. When I stopped and truly noticed them as individuals, I saw businessmen with iPhones, women with laptops, farmers wearing overalls, and teenagers with pop magazines all trudging toward the same goal. Some sported wigs or bandanas, some navigated wheelchairs or canes, while others looked like they would be seeing St. Peter by suppertime. But the presence of these unnamed people in my life was a huge factor in my own recovery, simply for their low-key way of looking to their left or right and being a source of inspiration to the person next to them. Though my circumstances were not yet changing, my entire outlook on life was.

A neighbor of mine, who is now on the music faculty of a local college, once told me that we will rarely hear the songs of the most beautiful voices, for they are not found on a performance stage. "They are in their backyards, planting flowers," she said. I have always remembered that quote. It summarizes so well what I saw daily in my journey: heroes who do not reside on the front page of the paper or occupy a spot on TV. They are sitting right there in the waiting room next to you supporting a family, loving their children, stretching a checkbook, doing good for a neighbor, and offering a word of hope to someone like me.

Of course, not everyone offers hope or a word of encouragement. Far from it—people can say the darndest things to you when you are sick. I define them categorically:

The Self-righteous: "Some people believe cancer is God's way of punishing us for sins, but I don't believe that. And you shouldn't either. I mean you don't have reason to, do you?"

The Easy-way-out: "You know, Paula; this is God's will for you."

The Insensitive: "Did you see the special on *Sixty Minutes* about how many people die of colon cancer each year?"

The Unwanted Mentor: "You need to eat right and exercise. I'm going to help you quit all of your bad habits. You need an entirely different lifestyle."

The Uninformed: "Did you know that every time you are put to sleep you lose tons of brain cells? They don't come back, either!"

I could go on and on. I learned that it is easier to simply smile and accept the comments of others, as I believe they are intended as a means for people to contribute something to your healing. Though I may cringe at other's theology or stagger at their erroneous advice, my view is that they are struggling, too, trying hard to summon up something to say to make you feel better.

And so it was one week toward the end of my treatments as I was leaving the office that, looking out the window of my friend's car, I noticed the same imprint that rests on all vehicles' rearview mirrors: "Objects in mirror are closer than they appear."

Then, in the span of a moment, every road, path, and rut I had traveled since that day in November converged. "Welcome, Paula. You are entering Damascus." An uneven, roughshod asphalt exit ramp behind the radiation clinic became my own Damascus Road that day. Why in the world should I be surprised? The God I had come to know in my life rarely operated differently. He always communicates the mightiest of messages in the most unadorned road signs.

"Closer than they appear." It's true. My objects were indeed closer than they appeared. In fact, I was tripping all over them. The objects of my affection, the object of my faith, the objects of my growth, all were looming in my "rear" view mirror. My very own "derriere" mirror!

As I took my Socratic stance and examined my six-month dance with cancer, I was overwhelmed at the growth I had experienced, all from object lessons that were closer than they appeared:

My desire to be an adult, painfully conquering the little reticent girl who looked to others to save her, was met when I was tossed the keys and given command of a vehicle that I did not want to drive to a place I did not want to go.

My cascading of an old value system and the erecting of a new one came from lying on a radiation table and summoning up entries for an internal gratitude journal.

My recognition of, and appreciation for, the true heroes of our world was confirmed as I sat next to them in waiting rooms and chemo clinics, watching them take on the ignominy of disease with the greatest of grace.

My vanity and pride were quickly replaced, not so much by my embarrassment in dealing with a cancer in a less-than-desirable location, but by the realization that holiness can be discovered on the rutted roads of life, not just on the pretty ones.

My tendency to see the other side of the fence as always greener was replaced with the awareness of the field of verdant green underneath my own feet.

The people and places that brought salvation to my life were not in a travel brochure or a self-help book. They were right there in my home and in my own backyard.

God, who sought to heal and comfort me, was not in a cloud in heaven; he was in the lives of those around me and in the glances in my mirror.

Now on the other side of my dance with cancer, I look at what it has done "to" me; but of much greater value, I look at what it has done "for" me. I consider its intrusion in my life not unlike the other foe with which I daily battle: Parkinson's disease. Being incredibly healthy for most of my life, I had to take a hard turn when, at 46, I was diagnosed with such a neurological challenge.

When I am asked how I rise to meet such health impediments as these, I am quick to say that the redeeming fact is, "I do rise!" Maybe with a gimp of two, but I do manage to rise. I could never count myself as unfortunate when the same biology that is subject to demise is the same biology that has given me health and incredible living.

In Rabbi Harold Kushner's book, *Overcoming Life's Disappointments*, he quotes Archbishop Oscar Romero of El Salvador, who, shortly before he was assassinated, wrote: "We accomplish in our lifetime only a tiny fraction of the magnificent enterprise that is God's work.... We cannot do everything. But this enables us to do something and do it very well. It may be incomplete, but it is a beginning."[14]

I am grateful for the tiny fraction that I am able to achieve in this world for God's kingdom on earth. It is all God asks of us: the unique fraction within you and me, used faithfully and devotedly for him. I am convinced it is the fractions of this life that move unseen mountains and conquer unknown trials.

My office mirror still resides on a wall at First Baptist, though I have long since moved on from the administrative post I held for so many years. In my last months there, it still served its purpose of confirming that I had an olive stuck in my teeth or my wig was askew atop my slowly returning hair.

But the mirror I value most is the one that allows me to look back at the miles I've traveled on tattered, beaten, crooked, and pock-filled streets, and survived. It's the friend that keeps my focus on all of the glorious objects that are so much closer than they appear.

---

[14] Harold Kushner, *Overcoming Life's Disappointments* (New York: Alfred A. Knopf, 2006) 173.

My Experience with Melanoma

Bill Sherman
Pastor
First Baptist Church
Fairview, Tennessee

Having served in church ministry since 1953, I have regularly visited church members and friends in the hospital. My first brush with melanoma came in 1988. Franna Claypool, a delightful and faithful church member, had surgery. Franna's husband, Bill, Jr., was a first cousin of well-known pastor John Claypool. In Franna's case the disease unfortunately had spread throughout her body. She died in less than a year. I held her memorial service.

Just a few months later, I came home from a revival service rather late one night. My wife, Veta, met me at the door and asked, "Do you remember that bleeding mole on Donny's back?" (Donny, our older son, was thirty-one at that time). I replied, "Yes." She shared that the report from the pathology lab had come back positive. It was melanoma, grade 4. This was serious.

Donny and Melanoma

Thankfully, our daughter Debbie is a doctor. Though cancer is not her professional area, she was able to do a literature search and get the wheels turning. We determined that M.D. Anderson Cancer Center in Houston, Texas, would offer our best hope, so five members of our family—Donny and his wife, Teena, Debbie, and Veta and I made the pilgrimage to Houston. We met two excellent oncologists, Dr. Charles Balch and Dr. Sewa Legha who advised us of our options. As far as could be determined, the cancer had not spread; it was in Donny's lymphatic system. Two operations were performed, and Donny returned to Nashville apparently cancer-free. We were virtually Pentecostal and hopeful that the ordeal was over, but it was not to be.

On his birthday, 9 March 1991, Donny had big-time headaches and slept all night and all the next day. We wondered why. Upon examination, it was discovered that he had malignant tumors in his brain, lungs, and digestive tract—the melanoma had returned. The outlook was bleak. Immediate surgeries removed 90 percent of the brain tumor and the two digestive tract tumors, but the tumor in the lung remained. Radiation treatments of the brain followed, and when these were completed, we returned to M.D. Anderson for additional treatment.

In the meantime, at church four of our finest doctors pulled me aside. They wanted to help. They graciously shared that our family be prepared for what was before us. They offered money, time off, or anything I wished. Then they graciously said, "Pastor, we feel you need to realize that come Thanksgiving, Donny will not be with us. No one with this many invasions of this disease will survive the year." In an apprehensive posture, we made our way to Houston to treat the lung tumor.

We met with Drs. Balch and Legha again. They shared that only 30 percent of patients in Donny's condition responded positively, then added, "We do not mean that Donny will get well. We mean that it will hopefully buy him some time, for only 6 percent of patients with metastatic melanoma get well." There was a long pause in a somber room. Then my wife, as only she could, said, "Well, Dr. Legha, somebody has to be in that 6 percent."

The outlook was disheartening as chemotherapy began. Donny endured six rounds of terribly toxic drugs, and all of the side effects kicked in: mouth sores, hair loss, weight loss, and nausea. Veta stayed in Houston off and on for eight months, and

I went when I could. South Main Baptist Church and our Baylor friends wonderfully ministered to us. We are their debtors. Then, an incredible thing happened. After four rounds of chemo, Donny's lung tumor began to shrink. After five, it was gone. Dr. Legha ordered one more round for good measure. Donny returned to Nashville tumor free. Before he left Houston, Dr. Legha said, "Donny, you are a very fortunate young man." Donny replied, "Well doctor, I had a great doctor." Dr. Legha said, "Donny, I cannot take credit for your healing. Most of my patients die." Donny replied, "Nothing disrespectful, Dr. Legha; I had the Great Physician on my case."

Donny came home well, and Thanksgiving of 1991 was the greatest Thanksgiving of our lives. I hoped that we had heard the last of this disease in our family.

My Encounter with Melanoma

Fast forward to 1995. As I was putting on my socks one day, I noticed a small bump on my right leg just below my knee. I didn't think much about it. A few days later, I showed it to my daughter. She said, "Dad, you need to get that checked out." A biopsy followed, and Veta and I made our way to Fort Worth for the annual meeting of the Cooperative Baptist Fellowship. On Saturday morning the phone rang. It was Debbie, and she sounded worried. "Dad," she said, "you better come home. We have a melanoma, grade 4." I was stunned by the news. I pretty well knew what I was in for. I do recall that I thanked the Lord that I had the problem this go around rather than Donny.

My son-in-law, Doug Brown, flew me to Madison, Wisconsin. My niece, Cecil Sherman's daughter, had married Doug, who was a specialist in the PET scan. I was relieved that the full-body scan showed no additional invasions. Two operations followed in Nashville with a skin graft as well. The doctor said, "Dr. Sherman, you have a fifty-fifty chance that this will come back." I thanked him for his efforts and stepped into an uncertain future. All went well for ten months, then an examination showed a malignant tumor on my shin. Another operation and another skin graft followed. (By the way, if you have never had a skin graft, you have missed one of life's stimulating experiences. It will bless you!) This was the beginning of my playing hopscotch with this disease.

Over the next four years, with six-to-ten month intervals, tumors appeared beneath my knee, my thigh, and my groin. Various treatments followed, and surgeries and chemotherapy became the pattern of my life. Our church folk and Nashville friends were super, sending supportive letters and cards, as well as calling. A well-intentioned doctor dropped me a note that said, "Dr. Sherman, I'm sorry you have cancer, but if anybody I know can handle it, you can." I wrote him back, "Doc, you don't handle cancer; it handles you!"

Through my many years as a pastor, I had visited scores of folk with this disease. I thought that I understood their plight and tried to show loving empathy. However, when I was taking Interleukin-2, Velban, cisplatinum, and DTIC-Dome, I realized that I didn't have a clue! My beloved brother, Cecil, called every day when I was in Houston. Sometimes, I was so sick that I didn't have the energy to talk to him.

Finally, cancer backed off in 2000, and I continued to have quarterly to semi-annual checkups. All was quiet on the Nashville front until 2003. I awakened one Saturday morning with intense pain. The long and the short of it was that I had a ping-pong ball-sized malignant tumor in my abdomen on my ileum (where my small and large intestines connect). Honestly, I did not even know I had an ileum, but off to the operating room I went. Before the surgery the doctor said, "Dr. Sherman, I do this surgery regularly, and we will probably find cancerous nodes throughout your intestinal tract." This wasn't what I wanted to hear. He added, "We'll check things out while we're in there." I thought, "Well, now what?"

When I came out from under the anesthesia, my younger son, David, was sitting there. He said, "Dad, we have some good news." I said, "Lay it on me; I need some." He said that the surgeon had not found any cancerous nodes, the liver was clear, and things looked good. I breathed a sigh of relief. 'Til this day, I am cancer free.

What Enabled Me to Cope with Cancer

It has been sixteen years since my first tumor invasion. I have reflected from time to time as to how my family and I were able to make it through it all. I think I can sum it up with three words that begin with F: faith, family, and friends. Since melanoma was not new to our family, and I had seen how my son suffered, I realized from the start the gravity of my situation. I, like other pastors, had preached the all-sufficiency of God's grace for years. Preaching it is one thing; however, experiencing it is another. All of us prayed for healing if it was within the framework of God's will. I never assumed that I would get well or die. I just tried to rest in the shelter of God's love.

One of our dear, well-intentioned senior ladies called one day. She said, "Dr. Sherman, is it well with your soul?" I graciously replied, "Yes, it is not my soul that's the problem. It is this sickly cotton-pickin' body." I learned firsthand that the great promises of the Bible are true; I had sung "Standing on the Promises" all my life. That song is on target. I've been there. Without question, it was the mercy of God and the prayers of friends and family that brought me through.

Today, when doctors in Nashville talk to me, they all say that Donny and I are miracles. Medically we are not supposed to be here. When Dr. Legha released me from checkups, Veta took our picture. Dr. Legha replied, "Veta, send me a copy. I want to put it on my bulletin board. I don't have many success stories." To the Lord we are eternally grateful.

Family was another bulwark through it all. I can't say enough good things about them. Veta was with me night and day. Her ministry of presence was like a stream in the desert. Our three children, my brother, sister, and their families were such a blessing. They gave me an incentive—it would be worth getting well just to hang out with them. In tough times families can either get bitter or better. My family circled the wagons and fought with me. I will ever be eternally in their debt. Chemo grinds you down. You go into it like a marine and come out of it just barely hanging on. In such times, a wonderful Christian family makes all of the difference in the world.

Another strength was friends. When Donny and I were in treatment in Houston, the Baptists and Baylor friends came out of the woodwork! South Main Baptist Church provided an apartment that we rented. Keep in mind that we are talking about a span of some five to eight years that we were in and out of treatment. Our Baylor friends heard the word and came on strong. Anything we needed, these folks went the second mile to provide. Friends we had not heard from since the 1950s got in touch. Dr. John and Joan Scales invited us to live with them for several months during my chemo as they were close to the medical center. Then President Herbert Reynolds of Baylor and his wife, Joy, called and sent flowers. All of these friends buoyed me up when I was really at the bottom.

The same can be said of our Nashville friends. Since our morning worship service was televised for more than twenty-five years, all of middle Tennessee, northern Alabama, and southern Kentucky became aware of Donny's illness and mine. We literally received hundreds of cards and calls from Catholics, Presbyterians, Methodists, Church of Christ, Baptists, you name it. Everybody was so nice. I still bump into folks at Kroger, in the mall, the hardware store, or around town, who ask how Donny and I are doing. There is a ton of loving and caring people in this world. They have surely been a boon to us.

Finally, what does the future hold? I do not know. I simply rely on the words of the poet who wrote: "I only know I cannot drift beyond His loving care." That's good enough!

Sharing More Than Scars

Diana Bridges
Field Personnel, Cooperative Baptist Fellowship, and
International Student Advisor
San Antonio, Texas

Childhood scars are like souvenirs brought back from a great vacation. Some of my best early stories revolve around minor physical traumas that left permanent marks. San Antonio, my hometown, is prone to long dry spells punctuated by flash floods. When I was eight or nine, all the creek beds and low-lying areas in the neighborhood filled with running water after a particularly heavy rain. My friends and I thought a nearby overhang, now an impromptu pool, would be a great place for a swim. As I jumped in, I gashed my shin on a jagged rock. I surveyed the damage for a moment and continued swimming. If I look hard, I can still see a faded reminder of that day.

There was also the time a Black Cat firecracker went off in my hand, and then the incident on "Dollar Night" at Rollercade on the second day of summer vacation, which led to a long, hot summer with my arm in a cast. And just a few weeks later, enjoying the waves off of Galveston, I had a memorable encounter with a jellyfish. Given the choice, I would have avoided the injuries every time, but in retrospect, I didn't mind them at all. My stories both set me apart and helped me fit in. My experiences may have been a little different from those of my friends, but we all had battle scars and we experienced camaraderie in having survived these little dramas.

Being diagnosed with breast cancer at the age of thirty-one, while living in Mississippi, brought about camaraderie, too, but I wasn't interested in being part of that particular club. In fact, I resisted it with all my might. I had known people with cancer. Some, like my uncle, had had the gall to die at the very moment we were praying for his healing. (I was seven and remember the phone ringing just as we got to the amen.) I also knew people who had lived. There were plenty of them, but the shadow of recurrence seemed to cause others to look at them differently, as if they were on a furlough that might be cut short. Maybe it was just me who viewed them that way, but after months spent in oncology waiting rooms, I found myself both repelled by and drawn to those who had been forced, as I was, into this new identity as "cancer patient." (One of my clearest memories is of one of the several doctors I saw telling me I'd be a cancer patient for the rest of my life. I was devastated for days afterward.)

I watched those who were noticeably weak and ill and wondered if I might be like that at some point down the road. I avidly followed the cases of everyone I knew—or had recently heard of—with cancer or any other serious illness. Each one's good news was a personal victory and each one's bad news a possible premonition of my own fate. I truly felt as if my identity and medical outcome were bound to theirs in some way.

I thought about death, of course. My primary doctor said that my chance of recovery was very good, though the tumor was large enough to put me in the Stage 2 category. He also said, however, that if it were to recur, it would probably do so quickly. Though that bit of information helped my mindset in the long run, it fueled my paranoia for at least a year and a half. Each bump and ache was no longer a simple inconvenience, but a possible catastrophe that immediately set off tolling bells.

When I thought about death, my main concerns were the road that might take me there and the people and dreams I would have to leave behind. Nine months earlier, with the assistance of many, I had begun to direct a weekday program for international families. What had started as conversational

English classes had turned into much more, and I was eager to see what might happen next. I felt like I had just settled in and gotten started in the kind of work in which I could invest my life—and now time was a devalued currency.

I was haunted by the thought that my children might not remember me if I died. My husband, David, and I had a three-year-old daughter and a seven-month-old son. I was still breastfeeding the baby when I was diagnosed. He had to be weaned immediately, which was traumatic for both of us. He wouldn't take a bottle from me and screamed whenever I held him, so I watched others hold him as he unhappily made the adjustment to baby formula, which he'd never had before.

One of the challenges of a serious illness is making decisions about what course of treatment to pursue. I had less than two weeks to make critical decisions and couldn't figure out any way to squeeze medical school into the time frame. My friend Robbie, a two-time veteran of the cancer wars, gave me one of the best pieces of advice I received: Get a second opinion. If she hadn't said that, I would almost certainly have followed the advice of the surgeon and the oncologist I had seen first. I would have had a mastectomy.

At the time I thought of medicine as black and white, beyond the influence of philosophy, geography, or one's generation. What I learned is that many factors can affect doctors' recommendations, and since doctors are, in fact, as human as their patients, getting a second (or even third opinion) is often the best choice, if only to be sure that all viable options have been considered.

Even before all the opinions were in, I knew surgery was a certainty. The only question was what kind of surgery it would be. One of my first truly hopeful days was when we drove to Jackson for a second opinion. I had steeled myself to hear that a mastectomy was my only choice. I remember that I could see a cemetery from the exam room window. (What were they thinking when they chose that location?) Despite my fears and the harbinger of death outside the window, the doctor said that I was a very good candidate for a lumpectomy. Hope made a comeback. I saw the blue of the sky and the green of the pine trees again, and had an appetite for the first time in days. David and I relished a good meal before driving the two hours back home.

The battle for wholeness was fought on several fronts, the first being state of mind. I put the dramas away and watched old sitcoms on TV, my favorite being *I Love Lucy*. I visited with the many friends who came by and rarely went to the mailbox without being reminded of both friends and strangers who were praying for me. When the stress of the unknown got to be too much, I tried not to cry in front of my children, especially my daughter, who was old enough to know that something was wrong. Instead, I routinely took long showers and cried to my heart's content.

A common casualty of cancer treatment is a sense of normalcy. I was passionate about holding on to as much of my ordinary life as possible. I went to work every day except for the times, every three weeks, when I had to drive two hours to Jackson for chemotherapy. When I had moved on to radiation, I scheduled my appointments for the afternoons so I could be in class in the mornings. When I was teaching, I could take a break from my own issues and invest in my students for a while. It was such as relief.

I also prayed. I grew up in the school of extemporaneous prayer. You talked to God about whatever was on your heart— things you were thankful for, things you hoped for, and people and things you were concerned about. That way of prayer had always worked for me in the past, but in the early days after my diagnosis, I couldn't come up with a prayer beyond "Help!" I knew asking for assistance was perfectly valid, but I needed more words.

Months before this, when my son was a few weeks old, I had made my first visit to a Franciscan prayer center about forty-five minutes from home. I went on the recommendation of a friend who thought it might be just what I needed. I loved the quiet there—not an empty quiet, but one that was full of meaning. You could imagine that decades of prayers prayed by the Franciscans, and the Trappists who had preceded them, had seeped into the soil and were now part of the pine trees, the roses, and my favorites, the Shasta daisies.

I loved the small library and started reading about prayer. I had bought a copy of Richard Foster's *Prayer: Finding the Heart's True Home* (HarperOne, 1992) when it first came out, but it had just sat on the shelf. Throughout that summer and fall, I read it with a thirst to learn everything I could. The chapter called "Unceasing Prayer" was especially compelling. I was fascinated by the Eastern Christian practice of *hesychastic* prayer, in which a short "breath prayer" is synchronized with the breathing. It's a prayer of repetition, but certainly not the vain repetition that Jesus condemns. In fact, the most famous breath prayer, known as the Jesus Prayer, is based on the parable of the Pharisee and the tax collector: "Lord Jesus Christ, Son of God, have mercy on me, a sinner."

In December I was ready to start practicing it myself. Prayer beads are traditionally used in this discipline, so I went to a craft store and put a hundred wooden beads on a string. I didn't give up my established devotional practices, but added this to it. About a month later, when words failed me, I received this way of prayer as a gift, and I prayed it before surgery, during chemotherapy and radiation, and through the months of uncertainty that followed.

My eating habits changed, too. I realized that proper nutrition was critical, so I simplified my diet, eating vegetables and whole grains almost exclusively. I read books and magazine articles, adding recommended items to my diet. I've never really liked tomatoes (except for those in salsa or marinara sauce), but I read somewhere that tomatoes had properties that might protect against prostate cancer. Even in my fog of paranoia, I knew I wasn't at risk for prostate cancer. Still, I added tomatoes to my diet. I was experiencing a kind of diet purgatory, paying for my past food-related indiscretions with a new austerity.

One of my students, a woman who had studied both Eastern and Western medicine, brought over two-liter bottles and gallon jugs of different herb teas, all varying degrees of bitter. It would have been tempting to have said, "Thank you," and poured it all down the drain as soon as she left, but I learned that she and another student had gone out shortly after the recent ice storm and dug under the ice for dandelion roots to boil. Even though dandelion tea was my least favorite of all the unappealing beverages at my disposal, I was overwhelmed by the work they had put into their offering and drank as much as I could, thankful for friends who loved me in such a tangible way.

One of the great discoveries I made was just how large my community really was. I expected family to be there for me, and they certainly were. I expected church friends to visit, pray, and bring casseroles. Again, I wasn't disappointed. What was amazing, though, were the cards that came in the mail from friends I hadn't heard from in years and friends of friends who sent word that they, too, were praying.

The most difficult phase of treatment for me was radiation. The procedure caused my skin to be very irritated, and having to go to Tupelo every weekday was time-consuming. The six weeks it lasted felt much more like six months. Perhaps it was my lousy attitude, but most of the medical personnel in that particular office seemed competent, but aloof. The one, shining exception was the twenty-something African-American woman who called each of us out of the waiting room when it was our turn to be zapped. The way she said my name, asked how I was as if she really meant it, and smiled reminded me that I was a person, and not just the recipient of services at the local radiation assembly line. She wasn't a doctor or a nurse so far as I know, but she cared for me (and everyone else there) in a way that far exceeded her pay grade.

The international women I had been teaching for just a few months did everything they could to lighten my load. There was a knock on my door late one morning. Ayten, a Turkish woman with very limited English skills, stood on the front porch holding a small potted plant. My friend Dee, who'd been subbing for me that day, was right behind her. Ayten had communicated in no uncertain terms that she needed a ride to my house, and Dee had complied. They came in. Ayten, with tears in her eyes, handed me the plant and gave me a hug. Then she sat on the floor and played with my children. I don't remember a word that was said, but volumes were communicated.

A young Korean woman went with me to chemotherapy one time when David couldn't. She entertained my son until I was finished with that round of treatment. She and others came faithfully to class day after day, even when I wasn't at my best and the quality of the lessons certainly suffered. Finally, after the months of treatment were finally over, they and their families gathered in droves for what was perhaps the least surprising surprise party in history.

Having made it to the end of the prescribed treatment, the waiting game began. Did it work? Was I really past cancer? I wouldn't know for a while and I wouldn't feel like it was true for even longer. That brought on a new challenge. I wanted to get on with life, but was hesitant at the same time. I didn't want to re-commit to dreams that might get sidetracked again. I came to understand that dreams are generally lived out in the bite-sized portions of hours and days. Each hour spent with my family and doing the work I was made to do was living the dream. I stopped focusing quite so much on the future beyond tomorrow's lesson plans and next week's programming.

The major exception to that was the fact that I really wanted another baby. This wasn't a reaction to illness, but a long-term plan that had been put on hold. If you look carefully at the forms you have to sign before undergoing treatment for cancer, it's clear that fertility is often a casualty. However, I'd made it to the end and all seemed to be well. I knew I needed to wait for a while to give my body time to bounce back and to be as certain as it's possible to be that the cancer cells had really been banished. Almost two years and nine months after diagnosis, our second son was born. Along with the excitement of waiting for a new baby, I reveled in the routine check-ups and milestones of a normal pregnancy.

That experience went a long way toward helping me feel like I'd joined the human race again, but my perception was still flawed by a skewed vision of normal human life. During months of treatment, I'd listened to so many stories from those who were helping me. For most of the thirty days of radiation therapy, different people from church would drive me to my appointments. Many of them I scarcely knew, but the two and a half hours alone in the car combined with the nature of our errand caused people to open up. I heard about health crises, family dysfunction, and personal traumas. The stories poured out and there often seemed to be a catharsis in the process.

At the time, I was surprised by the amount of drama in the lives of the mild-mannered church folks who chose to spend these hours with me. Much later, I began to realize that what they offered me was evidence of our shared human experience.

The physical, psychological, and spiritual scars left behind on each of us were like the childhood scars my friends and I took pride in. They didn't make us less human or put us in some exotic category. We were garden-variety folks. Our experiences would forever affect us, but they didn't define us, and, in the end, we found common ground among them.

Cancer isn't a good thing, but in the hands of God the Alchemist, surprising good can come even from something that is by definition destructive. It's human nature to hang around with people who are like us. Often, the similarities have to do with economics, sub-culture, and education. Cancer introduced me to another group of people like me. I've prayed with and for people from different countries and faith traditions. I've had unexpected encounters with people who are unlike me in many ways, but alike in this common experience. Facing challenges of death and life together, our differences, though significant, are overcome by the magnitude of what we share, which is, ultimately, not cancer but humanity.

No Joke on April Fools' Day

Slayden A. Yarbrough
Professor Emeritus of Religion
Oklahoma Baptist University

My initial introduction to prostate cancer was the diagnosis of my father-in-law, Errol J. Lane. My wife's, Janis's, father was a farmer in North Central Missouri and a Baptist deacon. He always was healthy looking and usually sported a great tan from working in the fields. However, he discovered in 1979 that he had prostate cancer. He was told that the normal survival rate was around ten years, but he sadly lived for only a year and a half before succumbing to the disease.

I never thought much about the possibilities of cancer for me, since my family has tended to have a history of heart problems. However, Betty, my sister, developed breast cancer and in 1999 was the first of her generation in our family to die from cancer. All I knew about prostate cancer was that it was fairly common in older men. I found out later that one in six men develop prostate cancer.

In 2001 Janis and I both took early retirement from careers in education. We moved from Oklahoma, where I had taught for twenty-two years at Oklahoma Baptist University, to Denver, Colorado, for two reasons: major league baseball (the Colorado Rockies had joined the National League a few years earlier) and the Rocky Mountains. We bought a loft that was a ten-minute walk from the Rockies' ballpark, and became season ticket holders. We did all of the things that retirees do, including, as disenfranchised Southern Baptists, joining historic First Baptist Church of Denver, a declining, historic American Baptist congregation located across from the Colorado State Capitol.

A few years later, I joined a select prostate trial for men that studied the use of Selenium and Vitamin B. (It would later turn out that there was no significant difference as a result of either of these two treatments.) I had seen a television advertisement that sought volunteers to participate in the trial and decided to enroll with no thought that I later would develop prostate cancer. I simply believed at the time that this was a way I could contribute to the research. This study provided regular PSA (prostate-specific antigen) exams, along with the exciting digital exam that goes with it. These, along with my regular visit to my physician, allowed me to monitor my situation for several years.

My PSA dropped to around 1.5 soon after enrollment in the select study. Within a few years, a gradual rise took place but remained comfortably within the acceptable range. In December 2008, Dr. Wagner Schorr-Ratzlaff, my fairly young physician in Denver, who had a good personality and a ponytail, noticed the rise of my PSA from about 2.5 to 4.7. He suggested that as a precautionary move I recheck my PSA in January, which I did. The results showed a slight increase to 5.3.

I scheduled a recommended biopsy in early March. On March 31 I took Janis to the airport for a trip to Portland, Oregon, where she would hang out with our only grandchild, two-year-old Kellan, while our son Scott and his wife Steph rehearsed for an upcoming play in their theater company, Third Rail Repertory Theatre. On April Fools' Day, I received a call from the doctor with the results of my biopsy. The six cell samples on the left side of my prostate showed no evidence of cancer. The right side, however, revealed cancer in three cells. Two were almost negligible, the third further advanced but not aggressive.

My Gleason score was six. I, of course, had never heard of a Gleason score, but from information provided by the doctor and from searching on the Internet, I discovered that it is used to determine a prostate cancer patient's risk of dying. The score is scaled from one to ten, and if a person is going to have prostate cancer, then six is better than a higher number. I immediately called Janis and broke the news. It was definitely more frightening to her than to me. The loss of her father had made a definite impression in her mind when she heard the phrase "prostate cancer." Furthermore, she was 1,250 miles away and would be for the next six weeks.

Because I became aware of the cancer very early, I could take my time in looking at options. I scheduled an appointment with Dr. Paul Maroni, a Denver surgeon. Boy, did he look young. He explained the basic options: watch and wait; radical prostatectomy; robotic surgery (he had done a little more than a hundred of these procedures); external radiation; internal radiation seed implants; cryosurgery or freezing; and hormone therapy. He also insisted that I speak with a radiologist before deciding.

Several months earlier, Janis and I had decided to move from Denver to the Portland area to be closer to our son's family. By phone and e-mail we discussed my options. In early May, when I drove to the Northwest to get Janis, I met with a radiologist, Dr. Chris Hoffelt, in Vancouver, Washington, at the Southwest Washington Medical Center, located across the Columbia River from Portland. I had found both the medical facility and the doctor on the Internet. Janis and I, along with Kellan, made the trip over one morning. We had not told our son of the cancer, and we feared Kellan would spill the beans about our trip to see the doctor. He did not, and I informed Scott of all I knew before Janis and I returned to Denver.

My visit with Dr. Hoffelt lasted more than an hour. As we discussed my options, I came to genuinely appreciate his professional thoroughness and candor. The bottom line was that he suggested that surgery would provide more certainty than radiation, and he was a radiologist.

While back in Denver, I decided to have robotic surgery done in Portland. Follow me on this: Our daughter-in-law Steph's brother's wife's father, Bill Reiersgaard, was a pioneer in robotics, and helped develop robotic surgery equipment. Scott suggested that I contact him, and Bill recommended Dr. Brian Shaffer at St. Vincent's Providence Hospital in Portland. I arranged to visit with him in August when we moved our furniture west.

I immediately liked Dr. Shaffer. He took me through all of the options. He had begun performing robotic surgeries early and had done well over 250. At the same time, he did not aggressively promote the procedure nor make unsubstantiated claims for it. I concluded that surgery was the one approach that had the best chance of eliminating the cancer and arranged for it to take place on October 8 in Portland. Janis and I went back to Denver to finalize plans to move.

The surgery took place as scheduled. I requested R2-D2 as my robot rather than C-3PO, the nervous one in Star Wars (never hurts to have a little levity before surgery). Through research I learned that the surgeon sits at a console, the patient is on a table near him, and then he makes five small incisions to insert the instruments, lights, and a little camera. I was asleep before I knew I was in the operating room, and the next thing I remember was hearing my name called. Those who have had surgery in recent years know the drill. They got me on my feet quickly and checked me a number of times during the day and night, usually right after I dozed off. The next afternoon they sent me home. I really do not like the word "catheter," but it was in its appropriate place for eleven days.

Following surgery I went home, recuperated nicely, and on October 30 returned to Boulder, Colorado, where I was serving as interim pastor of First Baptist Church. In early November, I began to see blood in my urine. I went to my Denver doctor; he ran some tests and put me on an antibiotic. A few days later, he called me from his home on a Saturday morning with a serious tone in his voice, which was unlike him. He said the blood test revealed that I had a very dangerous staphylococcus infection called MRSA and that it was essential that I take all of the tablets he prescribed. The antibiotics worked, and other than a little incontinence all has gone very well since.

In a journey through the valley of the shadow of cancer, faith is always very important. My faith pilgrimage does not see God as the one who solves all of our problems, or makes us immune to health issues, or heals us and punishes the poor wayward sinners (for which I also qualify). Rather, our faith in God sustains us, enables us to endure, teaches us, and prepares us to minister to others who face similar challenges.

I am usually quite laid back and never ask the question "Why me?" Rather, I ask, "Where do I go from here?" as I appreciate where I have been and anticipate a positive tomorrow. Faith is simply a constant for me in good times and challenging times. And as I look for the presence of God, I find him in his people and in the doctors and nurses who may or may not be believers but who reveal not only skill but compassion, as well as patience with the patients.

I found great comfort and support in Boulder, Colorado. I was nine months, exactly half way, into my interim pastorate at First Baptist, when I received the news of my prostate cancer. The journey ahead was significantly shaped by my relationship to this congregation. For one thing, when I prayed for those with health issues during the pastoral prayer, I looked at their needs from an entirely different perspective. I was one of those facing such challenges. It was no longer praying just for them; it was now praying for us.

A second characteristic of my ministry at Boulder was that the collective church demonstrated a sensitivity that can only be experienced. The congregation and the leadership cared for me, supported me, and prayed for Janis and me; they also responded with compassion and action. Janis and I were in the process of making plans to move to the Portland area even before I received the medical report. We were trying to sell our loft in Denver and purchase a place in the Northwest, which we did in early May 2009. I notified Larry VanSpriell, chair of the church's Council of Ministries, of my plans to conclude my interim at the end of September (which was also the end of the Colorado Rockies baseball season, not that this played into the calendar decisions).

Because the church had not called a pastor, it began to develop a plan to find a new interim. Janis and I decided to move our furnishings in mid-August to make the transition smoother, and the leadership gave me an additional week off to accomplish this task. In late August, we realized that our loft was probably not going to sell in the immediate future, and we could use the ministry income, so I approached Larry for consideration of a new plan. I requested that I be allowed to continue on as interim, while Janis remained in Vancouver in our new place, and that I be allowed to take off the month of October to have the surgery and recuperate.

I was not surprised that the leadership agreed enthusiastically. This meant a great deal to me. I was having a wonderful ministry at this loving and caring church. Furthermore, while I did not expect them to continue paying me in October, they did so without hesitation. In November the leadership gave me an extra Sunday off, as well as a week off to travel to our new home for Thanksgiving, my birthday, and to see a play of our son's theater company (Janis and I have not missed a play since the company's beginnings).

In mid-November, Dr. Robert Ballance was called as pastor, and my ministry ended the final Sunday before Christmas. I genuinely appreciate the Christian love, the support, and the authentic ministry that this historic congregation showed to Janis and me—in the most liberal city in Colorado! I might add that serving and working during this time was an important contribution to my well-being. In a unique way, I was practicing what I was preaching by ministering and being ministered to by these authentic, Christian people.

Another serendipitous development was the emergence of a number of the members of the congregation who had also experienced prostate cancer and other kinds of cancer. It seemed as though every other week someone would seek me out to share his or her story. Each one wanted to help and wanted to assure me that I could get through this. Each one seemed to have a little different slant, a little different approach, and a little different influence, especially as I was trying to decide the choice of treatment. Without a doubt the response of these individuals was the most important factor in my choice.

Jack Fowler was the first to approach me. I had gone to visit him while he had a brief stay as a patient in an area hospital. I met him as he was leaving the facility. As we walked, he told me his story with prostate cancer and his travel to Florida for a new treatment with the "biggest medical machine" he had ever seen. Later, he placed a stack of about five books dealing with the subject on my office desk. I appreciated this so much, but I must apologize to Jack, I never got through most of them.

One Sunday morning, R.C. Parrish, an older gentleman in the church, shared with me that about twenty years earlier he and then his brother both discovered that they had prostate cancer. They chose radiation seed implants, and both had done very well because of it. This conversation gave me a positive view toward this possibility.

Emmett Hayward some years earlier had had another form of cancer; while I was his pastor, his cancer returned. I would call him on a fairly regular basis, and his spirit and encouragement contributed to the development of my own attitude. He continued living a normal life, visiting with his children, and he appreciated sharing his journey with me.

Dr. Dwight Neuenschwander, pastor emeritus at First Baptist Church in Boulder, provided a different slant. Dwight is about eighty years old, in great shape, and a good friend. Not long after I discovered my cancer, Dwight's PSA began to rise dramatically. Tests revealed that he, too, had developed prostate cancer, and we had a number of discussions of options, information, and decisions. It was good to have a friend traveling the same bumpy road. In the end he chose a combination of hormone treatment and radiation. We continue to stay in contact and discuss our individual progress.

Another member of the congregation who has been important to my journey is Vondell Martin. She has experienced cancer four different times. I could tell immediately after I announced my circumstance to the church that we had an important connection. On the many occasions when one of us would ask, "How are you?" it was much more than idle conversation. At church each Sunday morning, there was always a genuine hug that said, "We have common ground and we have made it another week." Vondell is a battler, and her strength is contagious.

No person was more important in my own decision-making process than Dr. Dick Cunningham. Dick had family roots in the Boulder church, and he and his wife lived in nearby Estes Park. Dick had taught at the Southern Baptist Theological Seminary and earlier at Golden Gate Baptist Theological Seminary and had experienced some of the Southern Baptist political battles. One Sunday morning, he and Becky showed up, and immediately after the service he informed me, in a very serious tone, that we needed to have lunch soon. At lunch a few days later, Dick told me his story. When he discovered that he had prostate cancer, his extremely high Gleason score was 9.6 out of 10. Dick chose internal radiation and, upon the last-minute advice of his oncologist, also received two external radiation treatments. Unfortunately, he experienced a long period of radiation complications. His most helpful advice was that if he had to do it over, he would have taken a closer look at surgery. He did not tell me what I should do, nor did any of my friends. But this conversation caused me to realize that I needed to decide soon what treatment I would take and when.

Because of my age, 65, my visits with the various doctors and friends, my research on the Internet (what a wonderful source of information), and my desire to completely remove the cancer from my body, I chose robotic surgery. The results were very good, and complications have been very minor. I might add that a pathology report on my removed prostate revealed that my cancer had increased to three stages but none had advanced outside the prostate. Twice Dr. Shaffer stated that I had made the right choice, and by the tone of his voice he really meant it. I continue to have PSA draws, and the number continues to be "0", as it should be. Hooray for R2-D2!

I might add how much I really appreciate Medicare, which I paid into for many, many years, and the Medigap supplemental policy that Oklahoma Baptist University provides its retirees. I am amazed at the cost of medical care. My hospital bill alone was approximately $28,000 for a day and a half. Medicare and Medigap paid it all. So, thank you Uncle Sam, and as we sing on Bison Hill, "God bless OBU!"

The bottom line is that I, like so many others, can now call myself a cancer survivor. But I am well aware that none of us gets to this stage alone. The expertise of great physicians and medical staff, faith in the Great Physician, the ministry of ordinary people showing extraordinary compassion and support, the love of family and friends, and even the availability of good health insurance along with information on the Internet do not go unnoticed. So, I simply conclude that I am a survivor, and fortunately I am a good statistic.

The Chemotherap-ista Reports

Kelly Belcher
Baptist Minister for Twenty-five Years
Resides in Spartanburg, South Carolina

During chemotherapy treatment for breast cancer, I decided to send my friends and family a series of e-mail reports. I wanted to keep them updated about my progress, to reassure them that I was alright, and to address our collective despair and fear about one of the scariest processes in the medical world. Creating the name Chemotherap-ista seemed to cut the monster down to manageable size for us all. The following are excerpts from the reports, which began days following my first surgery.

There is Life Two Days after Bi-Lateral Mastectomy Surgery
26 August 2010
Dear friends,

A quick note to let you know that I am home and can sit at the computer, which means the official score is now Me: 1, Breast Cancer: 0.

I'll wait until Tuesday for the pathology report, which we hope will confirm what we expect, that tissue taken from my right breast truly is DCIS, or ductal carcinoma in situ, early and non-invasive pre-cancer, and that it is now gone for good! So please keep those prayers going for another week.

I need to stay very still for a couple of weeks. Sadly, I must forego my favorite hobby, vacuuming. I appreciate your prayers and good wishes, which were a wonderful thought to hold in mind as they put the anesthesia mask over my face.

Love,

Kelly

The pathology report revealed not DCIS, but stage 1 ductal cancer on the right side that had not spread to any lymph nodes. It also revealed stage 1 lobular cancer on the left side that was more invasive but had not been anticipated. Surgeons hadn't removed or tested the left lymph nodes since that was not the standard of care in prophylactic breast removal. So I was faced with a choice: permanent damage to my arm by taking those nodes for testing, or a course of chemotherapy, which would be the treatment if those nodes tested positive. Having the chemo, whose effects seemed temporary to me, meant saving the arm from permanent weakness. I chose chemo.

And There Was Evening and There Was Morning, the First Day
Monday, 4 October 2010
Hey friends!
You might want to receive this and you might not! People are curious about chemotherapy, and some wanted a treatment update. I had my first treatment this morning. Open vein, pour in poison, go wild killing off cancer cells. Now the official score is Me: 2, Breast Cancer: 0. Hey, I'm already doing better than some ACC basketball teams I used to like.

I had no adverse reaction to the infusion, so I shouldn't have one during subsequent treatments, according to my nurse. With platelet donations at the blood bank, I am accustomed to sitting at a machine for a couple of hours. Today I was just receiving, which is easier than the platelet centrifuge where they take a bit, swirl it around and give it back, only colder, with no platelets and just a dash of your soul removed. My platelet count is high and today all my blood counts were stratospheric, which I attribute to good genes (thanks, Mom and Dad), good nutrition, vitamins, and a little chocolate and wine for good measure. My apologies to the teetotalers in the e-mail list: I've outed myself.

The infusion begins with saline to which some Decadron is added. This is a corticosteroid that buffers the side effects of the "py-zon," as my husband Philip calls it. Then some anti-nausea medicine is added. Only then is the first drug started. I had a course of two, one for an hour and one for a half hour, and felt nothing.

We brought a pizza home for lunch. My instructions are that if I am to experience "unpleasantness," a way to name all the stuff you are already thinking, it will hit around evening and last 24 to 48 hours. There's no telling what will happen, but I already got my pizza while the good times were still rolling.

The word chemotherapy is as scary to us as cancer. We associate it with, well, death. It's horrible for people who must have long, bitter courses of it. We think of bald, scrawny, sick people. I have learned that this is only part of what it can be. The severity depends on the location in the body of the particular cancer, the patient's general health, the length and strength of the chemicals, and the number of treatments in quick succession. It is the disease, not the treatment, which causes the problem. I know some smashingly wonderful chemo patients who give me a calm, empowered feeling, and I hope to do as well as they have. I think of the treatment as my friend; our common enemy is the cancer cell that could be lurking. Since only the Shadow knows and doctors can't be sure, chemo is the best way to feel I am clean (well, from cancer anyway; I'm not saying anything else). So when the treatment goes in I think of getting something healing for me but weapons of mass destruction for cancer cells.

Some cancer patients have difficulty from the start, but I was lucky. I expect I can do three more of these and live to tell gross and humiliating jokes about it. In 72 hours I will know how I respond fully. Maybe I will change my tune. Maybe I will be only humming. Maybe I will just be calling Philip names. As long as I can vacuum I will feel okay. That's my barometer.

Thank you for your prayers. I'm an equal-opportunity interfaith prayer subject, so go wild! Thanks for good wishes and general positive energy sent my way. That is the strongest anti-cancer treatment I know. Yesterday I had World Communion bread and cup served to me by my woman pastor. I am part of the body of Christ, so there is nothing to fear.

Sun's out, breeze is cool, house is quiet, our bluetick coonhound's asleep in the grass.

Love,
Kelly

Friday, 8 October 2010
Hey there friends,

Your Chemo Correspondent here with an update on the progress of chemotherapy: we have had gorgeous weather and I've been outside getting my vitamin D and rolling in the grass with the dog. Okay, she did most of the actual rolling.

I report gladly that the days following treatment have been easier than expected. The steroid Decadron must be the reason there has been no "unpleasantness" for me. One might never know where the blessing of steroids could be invisibly working for the betterment of someone … but I'm not naming any national leaguers.

The chemo nurse outlined some side effects I might expect during the first week, but what I experienced was different. There's a strange feeling I find hard to describe. It's as if something has clamped down on my ability to be myself. It is partly fatigue and partly a sense that the electrical lines are down and the power is temporarily off. I can move around but only in slow motion. Sometimes it's reverse. I'm awake but it's not really me in here. I'm with Neo and Morpheus in the Matrix. We've kept walking the dog two miles per day and regular exercise helps. Fatigue peaked Thursday and today is a bit better.

The second surprise seems a contradiction: on Tuesday night I never fell asleep. The Decadron caused this, too, giving brief periods of extraordinary energy mixed with fatigue for a few hours at a time those first days. I could not sit still so I cleaned the whole house. My nurse said she'd rather have me cleaning bathrooms than fraternizing with children, little virus and germ carriers. So I minded her. There's nothing like quality vacuum time to wind down and relax! The chemo nurse was used to hearing this too and gave me a sleeping pill.

The final surprise is that I have to look into the mirror to confirm there is still a tongue in my mouth. I know there's a muscle there, but it has no taste buds left on it. It forgot tongue-ness. It just lies there with amnesia. Folks have given us delectable food that I have carefully passed over this tongue only to have it neglect to register any sensation whatsoever. I must confess woefully that chocolate has no flavor. I know this is treason! Forgive me! Horribly, wine tastes like kiddie juice. And it's the expensive six-dollar bottle too. If they'd warned me about this I might have reconsidered the whole life/death thing! Even water tastes as if it spent time inside a car engine before I drink it. It's hard to stay nourished. My immune system is getting down to Defcon 1 levels. Mashed potatoes are my new favorite dish, with mustard.

Within a week I should feel better energy and get back to some sort of normal. Perhaps taste will return but perhaps not until the end of therapy. The next strange sensation will be on my scalp because my Dead Hair Walking has only days to live at this point. I can expect to feel tingly or tender as that process occurs. The next time you see me you won't recognize me due to my glamorous new wig of indeterminate color, style, and length.

My new philosophy is that any day you wake up and have actual hair is a good hair day.

I want to remind you that this is Breast Cancer Awareness Month. Now friends, I am aware. Our collective awareness exists at optimal levels. But be aware not just of taking care of yourself and getting screened. I learned firsthand that mammography is not foolproof, and many important things go undetected while many false positives scare women daily. So be engaged in your own health. Do the right things for yourself.

Most of all, be aware of people who truly suffer with cancer, since most of them are shut away from the rest of us. Lazy immune systems force their isolation. Take some time to send a card or make a phone call to someone with cancer who lives lonely. Just don't call me, okay? I'm either vacuuming or sleeping. I mean for you to call people who are really suffering. I'm lucky; I'm not in that group … yet!

Many thanks for your interfaith prayers and well wishes. Love and friendship are soothing, wonderful things. It's eighty degrees, there's free vitamin D everywhere for the taking, the coonhound has a treat so she will not bark at the trash truck, it's a good hair day, bidden or unbidden, God is present. So bid.

Love,
Kelly

19 October 2010
Friends,

Your Chemo Correspondent here with the week's update: I'm in the Army now, and got my official Army haircut with just a dash extra to boot. The Chemo nurse said that people typically begin losing their hair about two weeks after the first treatment. For me that was Monday. On Sunday afternoon I noticed that a lot of hair came out on the hairbrush. It was also around my shoulders, down in my sweater, and all over the floor, which you'd agree is not typical. It has historically been Philip who can blow-dry his hair and end up with more sticking to the wall than his head. The fuzzy wallpaper look hasn't been in style for home decor since at least the 1890s, and the hairy carpet look is equally unfashionable, especially for tile. I knew I had to do something. So I decided never to brush my hair again.

On Monday I thought I'd do a real test. I ran my hand through my hair and grabbed a glob of it. Pulled it right out, no pain, no resistance. You haven't lived until you've seen a wad of your own personal former hair lying in your hand like a dead mouse. Or a troll doll.

Monday night I made the mistake of attempting to wash my hair. I wet my head. I put the shampoo in my hands and then put my hands on my head. I moved my hands from my forehead to my neck. Something was very wrong. I looked at my hands, which looked as hairy as if I were Bigfoot. (He's not a myth, he's just a chemo patient!) And then like an idiot I did it again. What hair was left was not going to get very clean. Most of it was already on the shower floor. Boy, I had way too much shampoo.

I had a tangled mess to comb through, and there is no more efficient combing effort than one in which you just take the tangle out with the comb and don't have to untangle it at all. By the time my shampoo adventure was complete, half of my hair was in the wastebasket.

The other half I had my stylist shave off today. She cried. She's a good friend, and I'm not exactly going to be her best customer for the next few months, am I? It only took a couple minutes and all that horrible dead hair was gone. I was relieved. She took some good photos during the process that I will show you later.

The big news: I have a gorgeous head! It's perfectly shaped and beautiful. I look better bald than with hair. I had thought I'd look a lot like my dad who is a look-alike for Clint Eastwood, because our facial features are similar and his comb-over days are pretty much over. No offense, Dad, but I look way better than you, good-looking though you are.

I have on my new wig of indeterminate color, length, and style, and when I went through the grocery store, nobody stared. Imagine that? I'm not the alien weirdo I had thought I might be. Well, I probably am, but it's not visible to strangers, as is the case with most weirdos. My eyebrows, eyelashes, and those little nose hairs in there are as doomed as my head. The growing back usually starts at the end of therapy, but it can start earlier. No matter what, you only lose your hair once.

I learned today that we have some wacky ideas about beauty. We think it is more important to us than it actually is. We are concerned with the way we look from the time we're old enough to know what a mirror is. Adolescence convinces us all that we are hideous. Adulthood can bring a mediocre resignation that this is the best we are going to do, but also the worst. Until middle age, when everything we had learned to hate about ourselves starts to wrinkle and slide down a few inches, and alas, over to the side. Then we hate it more and long sentimentally for what it was and where it was that we hated before. Suddenly we have a whole drawer dedicated to Spanx.

I can talk big because my hair will return and I will look the same again. It won't be "No boobs, No hair, No service" forever. But I think beauty is different now. I think of many beautiful people who might not ever win a contest. I think of my grandmothers' faces, images from when they were about my current age, and I consider them beautiful. I hope I can look like them one day. One day a long time from now. I am sure that if I could see them and they saw me as I am now, they would find me beautiful as well, once they wiped the overdone eye makeup off me. It is love that makes all of us beautiful, and any other standard is just silly.

So give a hug and a kiss to the people you find beautiful who are near enough to grab. Look how great their hair looks! Don't take them for granted. Don't take yourself for granted.

Thanks for your wonderful messages. All of you are beautiful to me. The air is cool, the tea olives smell wonderful, the coonhound is whining for supper and needs a walk, and there are beautiful people all around you, full of a divine spirit of love. If anything is beautiful, think on that.

Love,

Kelly

28 October 2010

Your Chemo Queen here with an update after the second treatment. This brings the official score to Me: 3, Breast Cancer: still a big fat zero. Half finished! As one friend said in French, you will forgive, we're "kicking cancer's ass."

It was just me and a bunch of old guys in the chemo suite this morning. I feel as if I have broken in on a Geezer Rotary club meeting when I see them, golf hats and everything. Even in my current boob-less and hairless state, they welcome me as the relatively cute chick. They are very friendly. Good thing there's no hugging allowed.

My wonderful chemo nurse spent the last couple of years in the ICU, so it felt very good to have her experience lavished on me. The infusion went just as well this time, both bags of "py-zon." I discovered that one of them is a mustard gas derivative and the other is derived from the yew plant, which is poisonous. I'm taking my WWI doughboy helmet next time.

The hard thing about the infusion is that all the saline going in has got to come out sometime, usually now. I usually hit the restroom a couple of times in the two hours I'm pinned to the IV. I'm an expert at dragging the loaded IV pole across the hall and into the restroom, and becoming the one-handed bandit with pants zippers and hand washing.

Brown spots, which get rough and fall away, have appeared on my arms and legs. The nurse sees these often: pre-cancerous skin cells that might have developed into skin cancer but are getting killed by the chemo. Yea! We discussed the idea that chemo is actually a great thing with many latent benefits and everybody could use a dose one time good. A lot less hair would be walking around, salons would go out of business, but everybody would have lovely skin. You don't even know how beautiful your bald head might be.

My taste returned slightly during the end of last week, but it will disappear by tomorrow. Still can't stand wine or chocolate. Can't taste anything sweet. I'm planning a great Christmas eating everything I've had to do without.

The bottom line is that there are lots of things worse than chemotherapy! This week we have learned of the deaths of two young men who were friends. They were delightful young people, lost tragically at the brink of their great futures, good children of good parents. I am asking you to pray not for me this week, but for their families and friends.

None of us knows what will happen in the future. We live every day as if there are unlimited days ahead. My own children are fine tonight, but I cannot expect that they will always be. And yet I do. Five months ago I did not expect I would be a breast cancer patient.

So we must live with deep gratitude for this day, the present moment, which can be fully ours only when we are fully alert and present now. How many moments do we allow to pass without giving and getting all that could be ours?

May God's presence be real to you in the present. May God bless parents everywhere who hope for their kids' long lives full of meaning, joy, love, and good work. May God bless all children, those who can go the distance on the brink of adulthood as our two young friends could do, and especially those who can't. And may God bless each of us, cancerous and cancer free, grieving and non-grieving, because we tend to move in and out of those categories in a random way, and because every day we all belong to a divine spirit binding us into one body.

Warm and finally raining outside, trees beginning to take their best orange color, kids doing fine today, coonhound kissed me on the lips but don't tell the chemo nurse. In this present moment, especially in grief, we can say together because of grace that "all will be well, all will be well, all manner of things will be well." So be present with God as much as you possibly can squeeze out all the time.

Love,

Kelly

17 November 2010

Hello chemo fans,

Hope you enjoy lovely fall weather, which we totally deserve after the heat we endured, complete with leaf color and long walks in it.

Three, count 'em, three chemo treatments down and one to go! The infusion went fine, with my poet husband reading his poems to me as I sucked up the "py-zon" bags. Poison poetry. Many say the third is the worst, but it was okay. This directly contradicts the old "three strikes, you're out" rule. Maybe I'm just a walker after all.

Old hair is all gone! New silver fuzz popping up, could be permafrost. Nary a razor or shampoo bottle is in my shower. True navy showering takes about 1.5 minutes with no extra hair-type chores. There are pleasures in baldness that I never knew, and now I look differently at bald guys. They are keeping delicious secrets: the pillow feels cool and smooth against my scalp. I'm free of the frustration of errant long hairs wafting into my lip gloss. And warm water washing across my head feels lovely.

The craziest thing to happen to this Queen of Bald last week was meeting a woman in the store while I was wearing my scarf and not my wig. She asked, "Why do Muslim women always cover their heads with scarves, even though we are in America?" I gave her my best answer: "Well, it is a sign of their devotion to Allah, obedience and respect for the community they belong to, and a way of keeping themselves holy, no matter where they are. But you need to ask them yourself. I am not Muslim; I'm Baptist. I don't have any hair because of chemo treatment, so I wear a scarf to keep people from laughing at me." She looked at me sideways, nodded, and walked away. Maybe she was scared of catching something from me: cancer, sarcasm, who knows?

Philip said I am pretty much the same as usual, except for becoming bald and sustaining a marked rise in my capacity for sarcasm. The National Sarcasm Society called and invited me to become a gold star member. Their motto: "Like we even need your support." It is easy to be sarcastic in the face of the little injustices I am discovering in dis-ease.

Here's advice for people who hope to help friends facing cancer treatment or any other medical treatment. I can't shake your hand or hug you, much as I love you. It's about me, not you! You are as good smelling and lovely as ever. If you are one of those metro-sexual, elite guys who insist on kissing my cheek in some sort of wacky European-inspired coolness, I will probably swat you with my wig of indeterminate color, length, and style. Hey, my knees still work great. Watch it.

After treatment some chemo patients are hyped up on wonder drug Decadron. I must take a sleeping pill that might keep me under 'til noon. If you call me in the morning, I will either be too out of it to answer or mad that you woke me from the only rest I can get. Call in the afternoon. Or call someone who truly suffers loneliness and is elderly and awake at 5 a.m., doing the crossword and hoping for some attention.

Funny cards and phone calls are fine things. I'm not dying, and laughing puts my situation into perspective and cuts it down to size. I am the same person; I am way more than cancer or chemo. I refuse to allow these to define me. So when friends are not afraid, that is wonderful and holy. The hardest thing for me is sharing bad news with people I love. Knowing you are a strong friend who can take it is pure redemption. I believe Jesus calls us to be present with people in their worst situations, and to keep anxiety low by sharing humor heals both of us. I am sure there are medical studies to back that up, even if they are in Uzbekistan.

Chemo nurses approve my cleaning the bathroom but not being with children. A non-crowded theater or store is okay but not a dinner party where I will hug and shake hands and eat food made by somebody with sniffles who licked their stirring spoon. Sitting in church with the *hoi polloi* [Greek: regular people in church, or low life at Tilly's Tap Room] is a no-no because of the huge number of germs encountered there. This seems counter-intuitive and offensive. I hate that too since y'all can make some really good food. Sigh.

The whole deadly germ thing keeps me isolated until I pass the nadir point of the two drugs I get. One's effectiveness level peaks at seven days and the other at ten. During that time my blood counts are at their lowest point or nadir. I am at greatest risk during these days. Like an AIDS patient, I'm susceptible to anything. After day eleven, I am on the way back up to normal counts which are reached by about day twenty-one, when they zap me again with chemo. Since antibiotics work with your immune system, and chemo patients do not have an immune system to speak of, quick aggressive treatment is urgently needed. We must be careful to the point of rudeness in avoiding risk of infection. We aren't becoming ruder, just less hairy and more sarcastic.

In isolation I appreciate that you do not forget about me while I am out of sight. I'll be happy to get out of chemo jail and re-enter society at Christmastime, and no recidivism here, I promise. But I cannot imagine the pain of isolation for long-term chemo patients over months or years. We must be vigilant in attending to people who are isolated. I have a friend doing a long hard chemo stint and I think of her beautiful self while I write this. To be out in the world is a sheer luxury, even in Reality TV/Cholera/Wartime/Recession/Political take-over land. When you are well, have hair, and can dress and leave the house, even if you sometimes dislike what you are doing, you are living a life that is free, normal, healthy, and powerful. You are fully yourself, able fully to become what God calls you to be. You must not take this state of affairs for granted. There is nothing you can't do. There is no reason to put off doing something to change your life or another's for the better. Unaccustomed to disease, we forget how powerful we are as human beings in the world. Do not waste another day neglecting to act powerfully for what is important to you. Go out and do it! I'll be here at home, making a list of the stuff I want to do when December comes and I am normal again, and another list of the stuff I'm going to eat once I get a tongue back. (First: research tongue transplants.) You go ahead though, don't wait for me! Do it now, against the day the cancer radiologist should say to you, your tongue and your hair, "I'll get you, my pretty, and your little dog, too."

Let what you do include this: thank God for your one, priceless, powerful life. Remember the isolated and be present with them. Do one thing every day you are scared to do, but are secretly capable of doing well, for the glory of God. Do it, then tell a joke about it.

Cool, sunny, and lovely today, coonhound asleep at my feet, redwood tree in the front yard is wearing her loveliest orange-yellow, still can taste a little today though Carburetor Tongue is coming on fast. We are approaching our time of gratitude and we have everything to be grateful for, an embarrassment of riches, because we have the love of one another. Be powerful in your gratitude.

Next update: December 7, a day that will live in infamy, my last treatment.

Love,

Kelly

7 December 2010

Dear Chemo Fans,

A happy holiday season to you, for it has smacked us right in the kisser already going strong. Now that I've done with round four of chemo, the score stands at Me: 5, Breast Cancer: a big zero. Hey! If I were using tennis scoring, I'd already have won this game! And maybe I have.

Pearl Harbor Day brought three things: remembrance of a terrible moment of infamy, death, and fear; the premature death of Elizabeth Edwards from recurrent breast cancer at age 61; and my final round of chemotherapy. It was a poignant day because of the confluence of these things. My chemo nurse came into my room to take out the needle and brought pink balloons. The entire chemo staff rang noisemakers, cheered, and congratulated me as I walked out, saying, "Congratulations, graduate!" I got to ring a giant bell because it was the last time I have to walk out of there. Out in the waiting room where all my chemo peers were awaiting their treatments, they clapped and cheered as well. It made me cry. Those chemo nurses care for some of the saddest cases in the hospital, and they do it with grace, kindness, cheer, strength, and love. May God bless them all and empower their good work.

Now I am settled in for my final Undersea Adventure of Chemo Cousteau, a three-to-five-day feeling that defies description. Philip has wanted me to explain the underwater feeling, and I'm not a poet! It feels at the deepest time as if the molecules inside my body are coming apart atom by atom, and my skin is a bag containing goo. It's sludgy goo that doesn't want to move, and I have no muscle strength or energy. When I take a step, it feels like slow motion. Or one of those dreams where you want to run down the long hallway but your leg won't go out in front of you. Hey, it's one thing in a dream, and it's another thing when you need to move so you can pee.

Carburetor Tongue has set in fast. My neighbors, whose sister died of cancer last summer, are wise friends who keep me supplied with protein shakes that I can get down during the days I can't eat. I have not been sick even once.

This is a hopeful word to everyone who fears cancer and chemotherapy: it is not necessarily the horrible ordeal we imagine. Everyone has his or her own experience of it. My prayers and thoughts are with people who must endure long, difficult courses over months or years as Elizabeth Edwards had to do. This takes a terrible toll. At some point she decided that she preferred to spare herself the effects of constant chemo. So far I get to avoid that decision. This one course of four rounds has been so different for me than what I had expected. So be not afraid. If Jesus said anything, he said that. Be not afraid of the treatment you might undergo one day. It is a mercy.

And here's why. According to insurance billing, one of my treatments costs about $13,000. They don't mix the Taxotere or Cytoxan solutions until I have a good IV going to ensure I can receive them and they won't be wasted. As the treatment flows into my arm, I imagine millions of people worldwide, beautiful, wonderful women who belong to God, as I do, who don't know they carry breast cancer and will die prematurely because they have no access to mammography, surgery, or chemotherapy. It is a privilege to receive this medicine. So when I don't feel so hot I remember this miraculous stuff coursing through my veins causing devastating cell death inside me and wiping out every cancer cell that could be there. I thank God for my life yet to come because I am a fortunate recipient of this medical grace.

So try to stand there and tell me we don't need to legislate health care for every single priceless person. Just try it! I will swat you with my wig of indeterminate color, style, and length. Are our own lives more valuable than those of any other person? Can I deserve life-saving chemo and another woman not deserve it, because I have money and insurance? It's the silliest idea in Washington.

Now that I've gone 5 and 0 with cancer, nothing scares me, not the Taliban, not the anti-Christ, heck, not even the anti-Muhammad. I plan another surgery on December 28 to restore my girlish figure. Since the August surgery that removed all breast tissue, I have been sporting expanders, a couple of nice hard pointy milk cartons under my chest muscles, sort of like bricks filled with saline. They've shifted a little, one to starboard and one slightly to the port side, so they don't match. Can't wait to lose these babies! Does the idea of surgery scare me? Ha! Does the possibility of looking a little lopsided scare me? No way! If you comment on the lopsidedness of my figure, will I swat you with my wig? Yes! Do I notice when people look quickly down at my chest to check things out? Heck yeah, I notice! You just can't help it. Curiosity gets all of us even if it does embarrass us.

Does that scare me? Nein! Does the idea of having two more implanted surgical drains for a few days scare me? Well, yeah, now, that does leave me a little weak kneed. Those drains are like having another set of plastic arms dangling sharply from under your actual arms. You want to rip them out but they are sewn in so you can't. You feel like a bug with a set of tentacles. For the first surgery I had four drains for about two weeks, which I kept clipped to a lanyard. Boy, did I want to take off that necklace. Philip called me Drain-o. But these drains will come out in a couple days and by New Year's Eve I will be a new woman!

Thanks for your messages of love that are a balm, so pay loving attention to those who suffer and need to feel your spirits beside theirs, holding them up. I am grateful for the net of God's grace in which I feel like a tightly tied knot, and glad I'm getting stronger and can become less "take" and more "give" soon.

It's freezing and the fireplace is humming, coonhound has her red Xmas collar on, and there is an advent coming now as surely as it has come before. So open yourself up non-surgically and let the spirit of advent brush against your insides gently, because this is the secret of abundant life. Then brush up against somebody else and spread advent love.

Next update: just as soon as I can sit and type after surgery December 28. Merry Christmas, y'all.

Love,
Kelly

Cancer Cannot ...

Edd Rowell
Retired Senior Editor
Mercer University Press

Several Christmases ago a colleague sent me a list of some things cancer *cannot* do:

Cancer Cannot ...
Cripple Love
Shatter Hope
Corrode Faith
Destroy Peace
Kill Friendship
Suppress Memories
Silence Courage
Invade the Soul
Steal Eternal Life
Conquer the Spirit.

Over the past fifteen years, during which I have been battling this Beast in My Bones, I have learned that it really is true: cancer can do a lot of bad things to a body, but there is much bad that cancer cannot do—if we don't let it.

In July 1997, my younger friend, Marc Jolley, gave me a copy of the thirty-sixth-anniversary edition of Harper Lee's *To Kill a Mockingbird*. I already had five or six editions of *Mockingbird*, and had long ago vowed to (re)read it at least once a year and then to watch the movie at least every other year. *Mockingbird* is very special for me. Partly, I suppose, because I know the town, the people, and the playing out of the story that

Harper tells. Because, like Harper Lee, I was born and raised in LA—Lower Alabama.

Somewhat earlier, in December 1995, I was reading *Mockingbird* again for the umpteenth time. It was just before Christmas, and I had another miserable URI (upper respiratory infection). URIs had plagued me for years—I had at least one bout every year, usually when winter set in. Routinely, my good doctor, William Patrick Roche, would just shake his head and write another script for a "Z-Pak" to help me over the hump, and I would be "well" within the week.

Not this time.

This time something was added to the URI. I had an almost unbearable pain in my right shoulder—all over my right shoulder. I could not tell where it hurt. It just hurt all over. Dr. Roche was puzzled also. We did the tests, including extensive blood work, x-rays... the works. Nothing. Dr. Roche gave me some industrial-strength painkillers and sent me home with his promise to burn the midnight oil researching to find the problem.

That was the first week of January 1996. Ten days later, I was back on the exam table, hurting even more than before. So Dr. Roche dug in again. More x-rays, from every conceivable angle. Nothing. So, more painkillers and Dr. Roche's admonishment to hang tough; we will find out what's wrong.

I credit Pat Roche with saving my life. He wouldn't give up. He wouldn't give in. And finally—about my fifth-ninth birthday, 5 February 1996, I recall—he called me in for "consultation." He had tears in his eyes when he said, "I'm no oncologist, but I think you have myeloma. I want you to go see Fred Schnell [since the beginning, my primary oncologist] to confirm."

So, it was off to see Dr. Schnell. And more tests, including a full-body bone scan and—Lord, help us!—a bone-marrow aspiration. (Since then I've had three aspirations. I'd rather be hung by my toes and whupped with a singletree! I've never had a baby, but they tell me a bone-marrow aspiration is as painful … or worse.) Finally, a verdict. The full-body bone scan found the tumor that was hiding from the frontal and rear x-rays behind my right clavicle, and the aspiration confirmed that, indeed, there was something rotten in my bone marrow—which I have come to lovingly call the Beast in My Bones.

The name of the Beast, Schnell said, is multiple myeloma IgA lambda, and he put it at stage 2. Some oncologists "stage" cancers: stage 1 means it is there and we need to watch it [that's where Geraldine Ferraro was before her myeloma got mean and took her away from us]; stage 3 means "Get your affairs in order… and soon"; stage 2—where I am—means the cancer is not immediately dangerous but we have to control it and keep a careful eye on it. For fifteen-plus years now, that's what we've been doing.

When Dr. Schnell told me I had a cancer called multiple myeloma, I asked him what the prognosis was. He told me we still didn't know much about myeloma—remember, this was fifteen years ago—but from what we did know, I had two, maybe three years. I looked at him as seriously as I could and said, "No! … There must be something we can do."

"Well," Schnell said, "there are some things we have been playing around with [his words, not mine] that might control your myeloma. But we don't know much about the side effects or the long-term effects. However, if you want to try some of these new chemistries, we will do so. But, I warn you: while the myeloma eventually will kill you; these new drugs might kill you too."

What kind of choice is that?

I signed my life away, the first of many times over the years, giving the cancer lab permission to experiment on me even if it killed me. I don't know of a cancer drug that I haven't tried—and some of them did almost do me in; I've had two bone-marrow transplants (1996 and 2001); I've been a superlative "lab rat"—no brag, just fact—for the international myeloma research group. (They read my x-rays in Pretoria. No kidding!)

When I was diagnosed with myeloma in February 1996, it was rather rare, often misdiagnosed simply because we didn't know much about it. Today, myeloma is spreading like wildfire: it is the second most prevalent blood-related cancer, after non-Hodgkin's lymphoma. We know a lot more about it, and we know a lot more about how to control it and the wicked side effects that sometime accompany the high-dose chemotherapy. (I could tell you horror stories.) Since Fred Schnell took over my case, I have been blessed with a cadre of doctors and nurses who are fearless when it comes to doing battle with this killer cancer.

When I was diagnosed with myeloma, I had no idea what we were dealing with, so I began an extensive research program of my own. I've learned a lot. One thing I have learned is that myeloma is relentless, but that I can be relentless too. I retired (after thirty years and one month) in August 2010. From 1996, when diagnosed, until August 2010, I missed very few days at work. (In my first life I was a pastor [1958–80], then finished my course at Mercer University Press, thinking to help these Baptists get a university press going—two, maybe three years—and then go back to my real life.) During that time I have written another book and countless articles, married a daughter and son (our oldest daughter was already married), been interim pastor of several churches (three of them more than once), baptized the first of our seven grandchildren, and grown some of the prettiest roses in all creation. I intend to be around to baptize the rest of our grandchildren—if they agree—and to write at least two or three more books.

Let myeloma do its worst. It may win in the end, but it will know it has been in fierce conflict with one who is determined and ever hopeful.

There are, indeed, a lot of things cancer cannot do. So far, I have enjoyed them all. But say "cancer" to some folks and they panic and seem to just give up and give in. I've seen it happen over and over again. One thing cancer can do is beat the very life out of a person—if we let it. So far as I know, I have been living with myeloma longer than anyone else struggling with the same Beast. I intend to maintain that record by continuing to be a good "lab rat" just as long as all the oncologists in the world will let me.

By the way, when I first began researching myeloma, a nurse gave me a copy of a paper that had been prepared by a myeloma researcher regarding how to treat a myeloma patient—while he or she is dying. The paper began: "Myeloma is a routinely fatal cancer of the bone marrow." That "routinely fatal" phrase sort of stuck in my mind—like a red-hot poker! But the more I learned about myeloma, the more I realized it is not the myeloma that kills, but something else that the myeloma opens the door to—pneumonia, kidney failure, a staph infection, etc. Myeloma does its dirty work by tearing down one's immune system so that any passing germ can jump in and sometimes kill.

One friend was diagnosed with myeloma (the same brand as mine) about the same time as I was. Then one Christmas a few years ago, she decided to play in the snow (it was far north of Middle Georgia, of course) with her grandchildren. She came down with pneumonia. And died. Another friend, about my age and with the same brand of myeloma in his bones, decided he just had to visit a good friend in hospital. He came out with a staph infection. And he died. I could tell of many other such persons who died "as a result of complications of myeloma."

That's why I am somewhat—more than somewhat perhaps—paranoid. My oncologists tell me to stay away from hospitals, nursing homes, and other such places and to avoid close contact with crowds, especially coughing and sneezing crowds. So I keep a close watch on my lab results, and depending on the monthly report I may or may not shake your hand (or hug you if you are huggable). Some folk don't understand. They think I am standoffish, antisocial, when I refuse to shake hands. If they are interested, I tell them that I just can't afford to catch whatever they are carrying—and everybody is carrying something.

As one of my oncologists—I have a bevy of them watching over me—said, "With regard to myeloma, we don't say remission." But we do have it under control. (The side effects of the chemistry I'm ingesting are another matter—but I've got that under control also.)

Eighty-two "moons" ago, Fred Schnell (my primary oncologist) farmed me out to Winship Cancer Institute at Emory in Atlanta and to Dr. Sagar Lonial and company. (Winship has facilities we simply don't have in Macon.) I entered a program to test a new kind of high-dose chemotherapy. My wife (Dear Ruth) and I go to Winship once a moon—every twenty-eight days—for lab work, consultation with all the oncologists in the world (a myeloma patient is allowed exaggeration), and to pick up a supply of special capsules for the next regimen. I take one capsule a day for twenty-one days, then have seven days R&R (rest and recuperation) to let my body settle in for the next regimen. At this writing I am in the middle of my eighty-second regimen with this new miracle chemistry. So far, so good. I credit the best doctors and nurses in the world, friends and colleagues at work (when diagnosed in 1996, Marc Jolley e-mailed the whole office, telling them what the diagnosis was and that they should stay away from Mr. Edd if they had even a smidgen of a cold), church folks of course and family, but especially Dear Ruth and our children who watch over me like a mother hen. (And allow me to say I credit my own good sense not to panic and to stay the course.)

We may not find a cure for myeloma in my lifetime. (Yes, that Beast in My Bones is alive and well and beating on me.) But if we don't find a cure it won't be my fault: I intend to be the best lab rat the international myeloma research foundation has. (They keep telling me I'm their "poster boy"—whatever that means.) We may not be able to run this Beast out of my castle. But what we do here and now may help someone else down the line. That is one of my fondest hopes, and the one thing that keeps me fighting.

Multiple myeloma is a real and a really mean Beast. But I've got him by the throat and I'm not about to let go.

Dividing Time

Norma S. Hedin
Fellow of the Institute
Professor of Foundations of Education
Director of Master's Degree Programs
B.H. Carroll Theological Institute

There are moments in life that divide time—tragic moments like the death of a loved one or amazing experiences like the news of a new baby. Hearing that a tumor in my body was malignant was one of those dividing moments. Life would forever be marked as "before cancer" and "after cancer." While surviving cancer is a journey that is part of my life story, the moment I received the news is permanently etched in my memory in such a way that I can hear the words, feel the same feelings, and physically react in the same way that I did at that moment.

The days leading up to that moment were hectic—the phone rang as I headed out the door to board a flight to Romania for an International World Changers project. Consumed by thoughts of the trip ahead and the details of coordinating the ministry for the next three weeks, I was surprised when the nurse reported that some abnormalities had been detected on my mammogram. She insisted that I go for a follow-up mammogram scheduled that afternoon. Explaining that I was on my way to the airport and would not be back in the country for three weeks, she agreed that waiting for three weeks would not be a problem.

I processed this news for a couple of days as I traveled and met up with the team in Romania. The students arrived, and we were overwhelmed by the work and ministry. Troubling thoughts surfaced a few times throughout the three weeks, but I pushed them out of my mind because there was nothing I could do about them.

Returning to Dallas, I reported for the follow-up mammogram, still not concerned. In fact, I discouraged my husband from going with me because of the normal delay for reading mammograms. I was surprised to arrive at a Susan B. Komen Breast Cancer Center where the technicians would do the mammogram, and the radiologist would read it immediately. After the mammogram, I was whisked away to a dark room where my x-rays revealed a small mass in my right breast, and the radiologist informed me that a biopsy was necessary. Returning Tuesday for a biopsy, I would wait forty-eight hours for news.

For two days I tried to push this out of my mind, not even allowing myself to worry until the forty-eight-hour deadline approached. That Thursday afternoon I sat in my office at Southwestern Baptist Theological Seminary, for the first time acknowledging that I might have cancer. My heart was beating fast, and I tried to imagine getting the news. I played the possible words over in my mind, and my body reacted to the delivery of either good news or bad news. My husband had assured me for four days that it was nothing. I hoped he was right.

The phone rang around 4:00 p.m. on 27 July 2005, and the radiologist delivered the dreaded news, "I'm sorry but the tumor is malignant." With patience and compassion, she answered my questions. Instead of saying, "You'll have to ask the oncologist," she explained possible scenarios. I could never express my gratitude to her enough, because the information was so important to me in that moment. I hung up the phone and sank down in one of my blue wingback chairs, a gift from a wonderful retired colleague. Knowing that I could not even stand, I felt the support of the chair underneath me. I also imagined the support that I would need over the next few months, knowing that my life was changed forever. *I had breast cancer.*

But my immediate thought, and the thought that supported me throughout the entire experience was, "At least I was not killed in an accident!" That may seem strange, but I have experienced great tragedy in my life—the horrific death of one brother at the age of twenty-nine in a fire that destroyed my mother's home, and the unexpected death of my other brother at the age of forty. At that very moment, the thing that struck me most was that yes, this was bad, but at least I could go home and hug my family and say the things I could not have said if I had been killed instantly. I wrote in my journal the following day, "Even if this diagnosis leads to an early death, I will have some time to show love to my family, to kiss them again and again, to say things I want them to remember." Weighing heavy on my heart as well was the sense of responsibility to bring honor to God in all things, and to model for my daughters how to walk through difficult times. The emotion came later, but the cognitive processing of what this meant began immediately. I was deeply and oddly thankful.

My husband was quiet as I delivered the news, but we immediately began to take action. I did not want to wait until the weekend was over to know the plan. I called the gynecologist's office as instructed, and the nurse asked, "Who would you like to do your surgery?" It seemed like the most absurd question in the world. I had no idea how to proceed. She patiently gave me a recommendation, and we called the surgeon, who agreed to squeeze me in on Friday afternoon. The surgeon was a part of Texas Oncology, and she knew how hard it would be to wait, so she stayed late to see me. By the time we left her office, we had scheduled the surgery to remove the tumor, and we had discussed the various options based on the results of the pathology. My soul was comforted by her compassion, her expertise, information, and a plan.

Sharing the News

Once I knew how we would proceed, I told my oldest daughter, Kirsten, who had just completed her freshman year of college. She was very upset, but I reassured her that the tumor was small and we had caught it early. My youngest daughter, Kayla, was at camp, so Kirsten and I drove the two hours to pick her up, and I told her in person while we drove back. She was thirteen and did not really respond at all to the news, although she tended to deal with things internally. I called my mother and sisters and told them and realized that it was a shock for them. I remember thinking that I was glad that it was me who had the cancer and not anyone else in my family.

I also shared the news with a couple of close friends. My pastor called about another matter, and when I told him I had cancer, he was absolutely silent for the longest time. He finally said, "I feel like I've been kicked in the gut!" I realized that the words "I have cancer" may lift softly out of one's mouth, but the way they land on others is an entirely different matter. Each of my colleagues at Southwestern responded in different ways. I could not tell whether it was the fact that it was cancer or that it was breast cancer that made things somewhat awkward. One of my colleagues came to my office to talk with me, and we even laughed at how my thirteen-year-old would think I had ruined *her* life. I was grateful for the humor.

The surgery was uneventful, and as the surgeon removed the tumor, my girls sat in the waiting room. My friend and sister reported that Kirsten talked nonstop, which is the way she processes things; Kayla sat quietly off to the side, which is the way she processes things. My husband, Eric, was supported by friends and talked about sports and politics, nervously watching the door. Once the surgery was over, the preliminary report was that it was a very slow-growing tumor and that the cancer was not in the lymph nodes—both very good bits of news.

Days later, the final report was that the tumor was "stage 1 ductal carcinoma in situ." It was slow-growing and very small, there was no lymph node involvement, and it was estrogen-receptive, which meant there were possibilities for prevention of further tumors. After receiving the worst news that I had cancer, now I was graced with the best possible report. We had caught it early, it was not aggressive, and I would not have chemo-therapy. We later met with the oncologists at Texas Oncology and outlined a plan for radiation therapy for thirty-three treatments, followed by at least five years of medication.

Surviving Cancer

From this point forward, my identity changed. While others avoided conversations about my cancer, it was all I thought about. Recovering from the surgery and beginning radiation treatment served as constant reminders that something can grow in one's body while one is completely unaware of the deadly reproduction of cells. My husband wanted to talk about "anything but" the cancer, and the girls were busy with their own lives. I felt at times that I had to remind those I worked with that I had cancer. I wrote in my journal on 29 July 2005, "I feel that I have just added cancer to my already hectic life—another thing on my 'to do' list." I was struck by the realization that many people live with disease and affliction every day, and most of us are unaware and not tuned in to their struggles. I was grateful for those who inquired and expressed concern.

One of the sources of healing for me was to talk with others who were going through the same thing. One of the ladies in my Sunday School class was diagnosed with breast cancer as well, and we walked together through the process. It was frustrating to observe the differences in our care. She is an African-American woman with other medical conditions. While my surgery and treatment began immediately, she was delayed for weeks and months at a time. But I was grateful that we could share our journeys and know that someone else understood completely. In addition, when I went to the hospital for radiation, I met several ladies who were undergoing treatment. We talked and laughed and shared experiences. Watching them laugh and talk while losing their hair and having reconstructive surgery and undergoing chemotherapy put my experience in perspective.

Interestingly, one of the sources of comfort and healing for me was information. I desperately wanted to know as much as possible about the type of cancer I had and about the experiences of others. I spent hours on the Web site www.breastcancer.org. Some physicians do not want patients to read on the Internet about their conditions, but it was helpful for me to read the information and the blogs. I never participated in the discussions, but I learned a lot through people's stories. I was encouraged by the candor and the humor and the struggles and the victories. When my family had gone to bed and I could not sleep, I would log on to the Web site and be encouraged by the stories of other women with breast cancer. This particularly helped me with the side effects of treatment. I had previously had a hysterectomy and was taking hormones prior to my cancer diagnosis. With the cancer diagnosis, I immediately stopped taking the hormones, which created a severe reaction in my body. In addition to the forced menopausal symptoms, the radiation caused skin irritation and extreme tiredness. The Web site helped me anticipate these things and provided suggestions for relief.

A third source of hope and healing for me was the medical staff at Texas Oncology. From the phlebotomists to the nurses to the physician assistant to the radiologist to the technicians to the oncologist, each member of that medical team was patient, supportive, kind, gracious, efficient, and compassionate. I cannot think of a negative thing that I experienced in my treatment. Several times the radiation equipment broke down, but each time they would work around my schedule to make up the treatment. The radiology clinic was not near my office or home, so they arranged for me to come during the last appointment of the day on my way from the office to home so that I could continue to teach my classes. When I had billing questions, the accounting professionals explained everything patiently and clearly. It reminded me that ministry is not confined to the walls of the church. Like the staff at the funeral home who ministered to us during my brothers' funerals, the medical staff ministered to me in untold ways.

Another tremendous source of comfort and healing was my students. For fifteen years I ministered to, and prayed for, my students each day we met for class. It was a completely different experience to have my students minister to me and pray for me. I was blessed to continue teaching while undergoing radiation. While I had to pull back on some things to make space to be a cancer patient, I derived great joy and strength through continuing to teach at Southwestern Seminary and walk with students in those days. I was also teaching in a PhD program at Dallas Baptist University, and I taught my first seminar at DBU the fall of my surgery and treatment. That group of students checked on me and prayed for me and encouraged me constantly. They clapped and rejoiced when I announced that I had been declared cancer free. They still ask me how I am doing to this day. It means a lot to know that others remember and that they care.

One of my students said he was praying for me and for my "affliction." We don't use the word "affliction" very often, and I was intrigued by his use of the word. The next day in my Bible reading, I read the words, "It was good for me to be *afflicted*, so that I might learn your statutes" (Ps. 119:71). While affliction can mean punishment and misery, the Hebrew word is more related to "humbled." The Hebrew word for statutes is "engraved law." I would repeatedly run across these concepts in my Bible reading in the days ahead. It helped me to realize that while I was struggling through this trouble, the purposes of God were to engrave his laws and his ways on my heart. I would cling to Psalm 34:19, "Many are the afflictions of the righteous, but the Lord delivers him out of them all."

All of the time that I walked through cancer, I was processing the experience through my theology. The comments of others sometimes cause one to evaluate what she truly believes about God. One person commented that I must feel like I was being punished. That thought never actually occurred to me. I was forty-eight years old at the time, and although I had suffered some grief in my life, I felt that overall I had been greatly blessed.

Christian music is often meaningful to me. One of the songs I came upon during my treatment is a song called "Blessed Be Your Name." It is based on the passage from Job that says, "Naked I came from my mother's womb, and naked I shall return there. The Lord gave and the Lord has taken away. Blessed be the name of the Lord" (Job 1:21 NASB). It expressed the deep, abiding feeling that even though this time was difficult, I had readily accepted God's blessings in my life, so it would be immature of me not to also accept the struggles as part of his plan for me. On my better days, I would write, "If I could know you better through this, that is all the good I need." On other days I would write, "I want to give up sometimes. I want to believe—help my unbelief." As I processed these words of Job, it so happened that the Bible study lessons for the Sunday school class I was teaching were also on the book of Job. I encountered Job's story from a different perspective this time; I identified with his struggles, his friends, and his conclusions.

I cannot adequately describe the supernatural comfort that came from reading Scripture. The promises of God for comfort and healing were constantly on my heart and mind, particularly the Psalms from the New Living Translation. Psalm 30:2–3 recites thanksgiving for being delivered from death: "O LORD my God, I cried to you for help, and you restored my health. You brought me up from the grave, O LORD. You kept me from falling into the pit of death." Psalm 34:4, 8, 19, "I prayed to the LORD, and He answered me. He freed me from all my fears.... Taste and see that the LORD is good. O the joys of those who take refuge in Him!"

It has been six years since my diagnosis. I know that I am blessed because my life was spared. During that same period, my mother-in-law died from lung cancer and my younger brother died from a pulmonary embolism related to surgery for his lung cancer. I am reminded that each of us runs the race marked out for us. I am thankful that my race is not over, but even if it were, God would still be good, he would still be faithful, and he would still be on his throne. For me, the words "You will not die, but you will live to tell what the Lord has done" was a promise from God.

At the time of this writing, I am preparing for my annual medical tests—the regular reminder that I am a cancer survivor. It is always with some anxiety that I enter into these examinations. And yet, it is also with gratitude. I have had six more years to invest in my family and in God's kingdom. No matter what the future holds, he has done great things, and I am grateful.

Prostate Cancer and Ancient Philosophy

Marc A. Jolley
Director
Mercer University Press

Around 1999, my father, then seventy-one years old, was diagnosed with prostate cancer. Four years later, he died of unrelated causes. Too much smoking and too much drinking and too little exercise had led him to have a series of strokes throughout his later life, and he eventually spent the last two years of his life in a nursing home where he slowly died in 2003. He died on my wife's birthday, and on January 8 we buried him in Cleveland, Tennessee.

A little more than two years later, my brother Tom, was diagnosed with prostate cancer. He had surgery to remove his prostate and, six years later, he is still with us. When he had his surgery I had no idea how serious an issue prostate cancer was, how serious was the surgery, or how it can affect a man's philosophical/religious views of the world.

I told my doctor about my father and my brother, and so we kept a close eye on my prostate numbers.

At the time of writing this essay, I am the director of Mercer University Press. In winter 2007, we had plans to publish a book by Ferrol Sams called *Downtown*, a hilarious Southern novel. Sams was well known and a great supporter of Mercer. The book promised to be a great seller and would benefit the Press as few books do. (His book sold more than eleven thousand copies; a high number for the Press). One day, in preparing his book for the printer, he had an artist come and bring original artwork for me to view and use for the cover. The artist told me that Sams had saved his life. He had gone to Sams—a physician—regularly for checkups over the years but was overdue. Sams told him he needed to see him. When he did, they found a problem that was fixable, but if left untouched he could die. He looked me in the eye and said, "Never miss a physical."

The truth was that mine was six months past due. It was February.

I called my doctor but could not see him until early April. My prostate numbers were higher than they should have been. Eighteen months earlier my PSA was 1.9, and now it was 4.7. It was time to visit the urologist.

I had a referral and visited my new best friend. I could not see him until mid-June. Yes, my numbers were high so let's do a biopsy. Now, a prostate biopsy is just about the most un-fun thing I can think of. I will not describe it, but knowing what my father and brother had gone through gave me courage. I had the biopsy in early July.

They took eighteen samples. The urologist told me that they would have the results in five to seven days and that he would call me. I gave him my cell number and told him that even though we were going to Disney World the next week, he should call me no matter what.

Disney World, the so-called happiest place on earth.

One of the neat things about Disney World is that when they make a mistake they pay up. We had saved for this week and made a reservation for the Animal Kingdom Lodge. About three weeks before we were to go, Disney called and said that some remodeling was going on and they would have to move us. They moved us to an apartment on-site (and never tried to sell us time-share), and they gave us a partial refund for the trouble. It was a great place to stay for the week. The refund paid for all of our food for the week; it was a happy place.

On Wednesday, my oldest son, Patrick, and I went to Virgin Records on Pleasure Island while Susan took David to the Lego

Imagination center. After more than an hour, Patrick and I began our trek to meet the others for an early dinner. My phone rang as we walked in front of the Irish Pub. My doctor apologized but gave me the bad news. He hated ruining our vacation. I told him that I kind of knew I had cancer. I don't know how; I just knew it.

I hung up and grabbed Patrick around the neck. We went to meet Susan and David and had a great supper at the Rain Forest Café. A cup we got there still sits on my shelf for extra change. Susan was scared. David said, "Let's eat." The words of a seven-year-old are perhaps the most reassuring. Life goes on.

Cancer. At 47.

This is not a theological problem. God does not smite some of us with cancer. This problem was two-fold: medical and philosophical. We would have to decide between radiation or surgery, and if surgery, robotic or old school, by the knife.

The Medical

I still read books printed on paper and when I buy music, I buy the artist's entire CD. So, I went old school.

On 11 September 2007, I gave birth to a disease-ridden prostate. It had a score of 7 on the Gleason scale. In other words, it was a fast, aggressive cancer. The only complication was that I lost a lot of blood—nearly half of my total volume. My blood level dropped from 16 to 9.2. It was a setback of time more than anything else.

The next two weeks were spent sleeping in a recliner wearing a catheter. It was so much fun I could not stand it. The third week was spent reorienting myself to the world. After three weeks, I returned to work.

Now I had to wait for my next appointment in three months to see if the cancer was still in my system. I have now waited for four years and no sign of the cancer. One more year and I may be cured.

The Philosophical

One of the things that has surprised many people is how I dealt with this entire situation. "How has God helped you?" "Did you read the Bible? What did you read?" "Were you ever mad at God?" "It is terrible to be facing the end at such a young age. How do you cope with it?"

My responses? God gave me family and friends and intelligence (although many question me on this). No, I've read the Bible. I know what happened to Job, Jeremiah, and Jesus. None of it was God's fault. Although, recalling Paul's words in Philippians helped some later. I was never mad at God. I could never believe in a God who would smite me with cancer. The end? I'm not quite dead. There is no indication that this thing is going to kill me soon.

But on a day-to-day basis I did need something. My drug of choice was ancient philosophy (especially Stoicism): Epicurus, Seneca, and Cicero. Three weeks on the couch, on the recliner, at home with nothing to do but eat foods to help my blood count, watch movies, and spend a lot of time reading.

Seneca

Two essays by Seneca were pivotal in my coping with my condition. The first is called "On the Happy Life" and the other "The Shortness of Life." Here are a few quotes that gave me a way of looking at life in a new way:

> The happy life, therefore, is a life that is in harmony with its own nature, and it can be attained in only one way. First of all, we must have a sound mind and one that is in constant possession of its sanity; second, it

must be courageous and energetic, and too, capable of the noblest fortitude, ready for every emergency, careful of the body and of all that concerns it, but without anxiety; lastly, it must be attentive to all the advantages that adorn life, but with over-much love for none—the user, but not the slave, of the gifts of Fortune. You understand, even if I do not say more, that, when once we have driven away all that excites or affrights us, there ensues unbroken tranquility and enduring freedom; for when pleasures and fears have been banished, then, in place of all that is trivial and fragile and harmful just because of the evil it works, there comes upon us first a boundless joy that is firm and unalterable, then peace and harmony of the soul and true greatness coupled with kindliness; for all ferocity is born from weakness. (107)

Loving Thoreau, my favorite writer, it is from Seneca that he receives ancient wisdom about Nature:

For we must use Nature as our guide; she it is that Reason heeds, it is of her that it takes counsel. Therefore to live happily is the same thing as to live according to Nature.... Let a man not be corrupted by external things, let him be unconquerable and admire only himself, courageous in spirit and ready for any fate, let him be the moulder of his own life; let not his confidence be without knowledge, nor his knowledge without firmness; let his decisions once made abide, and let not his decrees be altered by any erasure. (119)

Early Christians thought Paul and Seneca knew each other because they had many similar ideas. Paul mentions on several occasions both the fruits of the spirit and works of the flesh. Seneca calls them virtues and vices. Seneca lists as vices things like haughtiness, self-absorption, a puffed-up superiority, slothfulness and many others (125). Some virtues are wisdom, temperance, and pleasure (only in the sense that meeting one's basic needs brings pleasure: friendship, diet, justice, etc).

The Happy Life for Seneca is about living a life of virtue. You cannot control what happens to you but you can control your response to it. Such a life is not controlled by others but by oneself. How I chose to respond to prostate cancer was my choice. I could not control the getting of the DNA when I was conceived, nor of having the disease, but I could control how I went about my life afterwards.

The person behind this philosophy was Epicurus. Christians have always hated Epicureanism. But that was not Epicurus. He was accused of many wrongful things because he was the father of the pleasure principle. Life should bring us pleasure. But Epicurus's idea of pleasure is much more in tune with Mennonites and Amish than with Bacchic Roman drinking parties for which he was accused. Epicurus believed that the things that brought true pleasure were not overeating, overdrinking, carousing, and self-absorption. Rather, his dinner parties included his best friends because friendship was the ultimate; he drank water and rarely ever drank wine; he ate vegetables and breads and almost never meat; and the only carousing he did was with his own wife.

Epicurus was the founder of Stoicism. He taught that the externals in life could not hurt us. What was internal is what matters. Cancer is not an internal, ironically. It does not determine who we are. It does not determine how we view life, how we love, how we befriend. Cancer eats. But that is its only power, according to Stoicism. Yes, the New Testament talks about faith in God and about being faithful in times of trouble.

But the New Testament only discusses the sick in reference to getting healed. This is a very surface reading, and maybe we need to look to other texts, like the Beatitudes for help. But Epicurus's teachings on how to deal with externals were critical for me and for how I approached my battle. Cancer did not change who I am or how I lived; it simply challenged my body.

Seneca says

Nothing shall I ever do for the sake of opinion, everything for the sake of my conscience.... In eating and drinking my aim shall be to quench the desires of Nature, not to fill my belly. I shall be agreeable to my friends, to my enemies mild and indulgent. I shall give pardon before it is asked, and hasten to grant all honourable requests. I shall know that the whole world is my country.... And whenever Nature demands back my breath, or my reason releases it, I shall depart, bearing witness that I have loved a good conscience and all good endeavor, that I have been guilty of nothing that impaired the liberty of any man, least of all my own (151–53).

It is no wonder that Thomas Jefferson and the founders loved their Seneca. Seneca—a good follower of Epicurus—understood about these externals.

Seneca sounds very Christlike in summing up how we look at and criticize others: "You look at the pimples of others when you yourselves are covered with a mass of sores" (177). Criticizing others is the most narcissistic of acts: it degrades the other to puff up the self. There is a temptation brought to the cancer patient that says that you have been dumped on, that someone, some god, or something is to blame. This is a poor response. The response we make to cancer, to anything, reveals our true selves. If we are Christians, or Stoics, we should respond with love and respect and not with hatred or anger.

Seneca's "The Shortness of Life" is a beautifully written book or essay (in the ancient world, a book was short, like books of the Bible, especially those of the New Testament). On the second page of the essay, Seneca cuts us to the quick:

> Life is long enough, and it has been given in suffi- ciently generous measure to allow the accomplishment of the very greatest things if the whole of it is well invested…. So it is—the life we receive is not short, but what we make it so, nor do we have any lack of it, but are wasteful of it (289).

Seneca lashes out at people who claim that they will do things of fun and pleasure and good when they retire. They have no idea how long they will live, he says, and, he adds, "What foolish forgetfulness of mortality to postpone wholesome plans to" the years you may not live to, i.e., retirement. Cancer threatens life, but as Seneca tells us life is not about how long it is, it is about whether we waste it or use it to the fullest. By example, Seneca, Paul, Jesus, and many others show us that this was their philosophy. Prostate cancer may threaten the length of my life, but if I have lived the good life (in the truest philosophical/biblical sense), then the number of years doesn't matter. It matters mostly to those left behind. This sounds cold but it is Stoic. It does not work for everyone, but it worked for me.

Seneca summarizes all of philosophy with this: "It takes the whole of life to learn how to live, and—what will perhaps make you wonder more—it takes the whole of life to learn how to die" (305). He concludes that only those who take time for philosophy are prepared to live their life (333).[15] In other words, trying to live without a philosophy—one you are willing to live and die for, says Kierkegaard—then you will find yourself terrified with cancer in your life.

Cicero

I read much more Cicero than I can communicate here. His thoughts on justice, virtue, and the good life (a virtuous life) were of great mental gain. But it was in his essay called "On Old Age" that I came up with a few kernels. At forty-seven I was hardly of old age. But, when you have cancer at forty-seven, you are not sure if you are near death's door or not. And, after all, old age is a very relative term. Growing up I thought, as most people do, that when my strength and hair left me then I would be nearing the end. Wisely, Cicero helped me here: "It is not by muscle, speed, or physical dexterity that great things are achieved, but by reflection, force of character, and judgement; in these qualities old age is usually not only not poorer, but is even richer" (27).

If my body was wearing out then I must emphasize my other traits, one of which is the wisdom to listen to these ancient teachers that there is more to life than physical dexterity. It sounds like a cliché, but it is true.

For Cicero, one should fight against old age: "to fight against it as we would fight against disease; to adopt a regimen of health; to practice moderate exercise; and to take just enough food and drink to restore our strength and not to over burden it" (45). But, he adds with sincere advice, "much greater care is due to the mind and soul" (45).

---

[15] Seneca lived what he wrote. He tried to be an advisor to Nero, and when he could not counsel the crazed ruler, he was sentenced to die by suicide.

The last thing I took from this essay was his statement that "surely there can be no greater pleasure than the pleasures of the mind" (63). For those three weeks before I returned to work and church, I devoted myself to these writings. Like I said, it was never a theological problem. I never faulted God. Why should I? Rather, it was a problem of "what now do I do?" These thinkers gave me some directions that I could not find in the New Testament or in the prophets. Job would have helped, but I knew I was not being assaulted by God or Satan.

After I returned to mainstream living, I began exercising, eating a little differently (but because I lost so much blood I had to overeat for a while), and taking things a lot slower—too slow, in fact. I had no idea how long the recovery would take. Some people told me it would take me six months to feel normal; some told me it would take one year; one person told me it takes eight-to-ten years for my body to completely heal.

I began to feel old.

About fifteen months after surgery and six good check-ups, I took a walk (as part of my everyday exercise); and as I walked, it occurred to me that for the first time since my surgery I had the feeling that I was alive. The feeling so overwhelmed me that I almost cried in the middle of the street. I had no idea how melancholy I had been. Doing the best I could with my philosophical armament may have kept me from going off of the deep end, but one thing was certain on this day. God's hand had touched me and renewed me. Or, it may have been more like a kick in the pants, like when God told Jeremiah that if he could not keep up with the runners then he would never run with the horsemen (Jer. 12:1–6). Either way, I had something I had to do, and I was going to do it, like the t-shirt checklist for today:

Beat Cancer
and
Live my life.

Sources:

Cicero, *On Old Age; On Friendship; On Divination*. Loeb Classical Library.
   Cambridge, MA: Harvard University Press, 1923.
Seneca, *Moral Essays, Volume II*. Loeb Classical Library. Cambridge, MA:
   Harvard University Press, 1932 (2001).

Where Is God in All This?

Lane H. Powell
Interpersonal Relationships Coach for
Individuals and Organizations
Lubbock, Texas

BC (Before Cancer), I often described myself as an excellent candidate for the Prevention Poster Child. At age fifty-eight, I was proud of my good health habits: low-fat eating, regular (honest) aerobic exercise, not overweight, normal blood pressure, and mammograms at the recommended intervals. And I had breastfed all of my babies. Truly, I had no risk factors that predicted breast cancer. Well, except for a high-stress lifestyle, and a moderate history of breast cancer (a cousin and a paternal grandmother) in my family, and a separation for twelve months from my husband of thirty-eight years because of an upcoming move and work commitments. In 1997, I was concluding twelve years of teaching and chairing the Department of Family Studies at Samford University in Birmingham, Alabama, writing a textbook, and coping with a youngest son who was having trouble moving on to a successful college experience. Who had time for cancer?

I had never had a history of painful breasts either, as many women do. But in the fall of 1998, soon after I moved to Lubbock, Texas, to join my husband, I was very surprised to experience pain in my right breast. It was soon after my yearly checkup and mammogram. When I reported this irregularity to my new primary care physician (PCP), she brushed off my fears of cancer saying that, "early cancer doesn't usually cause pain." She did, however, schedule a follow-up visit in six months. I even got a second opinion from a gynecologist who also said it was probably a clogged milk duct and advised me to use hot compresses and take a vitamin supplement. I followed his advice, and the pain eased. But a month or so before my follow-up visit to my PCP, the pain returned, accompanied by a rash on the right side of my breast. It was as if God were saying, "Look here; look here." I casually mentioned this rash to my PCP who looked at it and exclaimed, "When did this start? Don't ever let it go this long again!" She called her med-school mentor, the head of surgery at Texas Tech Health Sciences Center, for a consultation and an appointment for me. He felt "99.9 percent sure" it was a low-grade infection or cyst and not cancer, and prescribed antibiotics and a sonogram before my appointment with him. After reviewing my mammograms (which never showed a mass) and the sonogram and attempting to drain a cyst, Dr. Griswold concluded that he was not happy with the results. He wanted to do surgery to remove a fibroadenoma that was blocking a clear view of the right breast, so that we could be assured there was no tumor—or future tumor underneath. I agreed wholeheartedly, and the surgery was scheduled for two weeks later.

That was when the 2.5-centimeter tumor was discovered, apparently hidden under the fibroadenoma. The biopsy revealed stage 2 invasive ductal carcinoma. Bob and I did not know any of this until I came back to my PCP's office for an after-surgery checkup. The waiting room was empty except for the two of us. Definitely strange. When the surgeon, Dr. Griswold, arrived along with the PCP, I knew for certain something was not right. As gently as he could, he explained what the biopsy revealed. He was almost as puzzled as we were. I was stunned, and my husband looked as if he were in a state of shock. We truly did not expect this. Fortunately, we were sitting together in the PCP's private office, and I did not get the news over the phone. The surgeon explained that he wanted to go back in for a second surgery to be sure that he had gotten "clear margins" and to check lymph node involvement. He suggested that I read up on my options, a lumpectomy or a mastectomy, and call him if I had any questions. Ultimately I opted for the lumpectomy, if it was possible. I had read that this was just as successful as mastectomy, provided the cancer was not widespread. The second surgery revealed that I had no lymph node involvement, and Dr. Griswold was able to preserve my breast. I have never regretted the lumpectomy decision.

I am also very grateful that my surgeon advised me to see an oncologist before determining the best follow-up treatment. Apparently, some surgeons do not see the need for an oncologist's opinion on follow-up treatment, and that attitude cost the life of one of my dear friends. The oncologist determined that I had an 80 percent chance of non-recurrence with no follow-up treatment. He explained that we could "up the odds" if I did adjuvant chemotherapy as well as radiation. He explained that this was based on the size of the tumor and the fact that my type of breast cancer would not be responsive to Tamoxifen, a drug that can guard against recurrence in many persons. Although I was not keen on suffering the well-known side effects (nausea, losing my hair) from the chemo, the opportunity to up my chances of non-recurrence was worth it. An aside here: I could not have had two more caring physicians than Dr. Griswold and the oncologist, Dr. Cobos. They spent time listening to my anxieties and answering every question. And I had plenty of them.

It was about this time that I finally let go of the fantasy that I could control my life. I had been blaming my body—and probably God as well—for letting me down, after all I had done over the years to stay healthy. A new attitude inserted itself in my mind: "Your body is your friend and it will help you weather this storm." I decided to do what I could to give my body the best chance to resist the cancer and to heal.

I began to keep an electronic journal, which I sent to my close friends. I explained that I did not want phone calls, as reciting over and over what I was dealing with would tire me. Instead, I would keep them posted by e-mail, and they could write back notes of encouragement. (Cards and gifts were also welcomed). It was my own version of CaringBridge, the online support Web site for persons experiencing serious crises in their lives.

I also asked my friends who were herbalists if there was anything they recommended as a supplement. They suggested milk thistle to help flush toxins out of the liver and ginger to combat the side effects of chemo. I started taking the milk thistle supplement two weeks before my first chemo appointment; I took crystallized ginger with me to nibble on while the chemo was being administered. I credit both with keeping nausea at bay.

A sense of humor also lifted my spirits and helped my recovery. I "played with" my wig, once publicly pulling it off at the end of a marriage enrichment session Bob and I were presenting on Coping with Stress. AB (after baldness), I had a t-shirt printed that said, "I'm too sexy for my hair." I learned to love hats and bandannas and to "play the C-Card" when I wanted to bow out of some obligation. This was a time to take care of me, right? I also learned to have great empathy with bald men, who did not have as many options as I did to cover up a cold pate. Knowing that research shows that laughter boosts the body's immunity, I got permission to put together a book of cartoons and jokes for the cancer patients' waiting room. *Smile Awhile* was copied and placed among the other reading material.

I continued my university teaching and regular aerobic exercise with self-permission to quit when I got tired. I added "napping without guilt" to my daily routine—a serious change for a high-energy, hard-charging person like me. And I visualized myself "floating on a benevolent sea." I experienced a wonderful sense of letting go, relaxing, and letting divine energy flow through me. I also welcomed the breast cancer survivor visit from Reach to Recovery and joined the American Cancer Society support group for breast cancer survivors, which I eventually co-facilitated for five years. I also took upon myself "the care and feeding of the waiting room" at the Southwest Cancer Center. My complaints about outdated magazines, dying plants, and a moldy fish tank did not fall on deaf ears. I was asked to be on the center's patient advisory committee. Ultimately, many of the committee's suggestions were incorporated into a new expanded Center that now offers an environment of hope and healing to many cancer patients.

All of these decisions and activities offered a measure of support to me, but the most important source of support was my family. My husband, Bob, never waivered in showing me how much he loved me and telling me how beautiful and desirable I still was, bald head, swollen feet, lopsided breasts, and all. My adult children and sisters called and made time for visits from their long-distance homes. My son, a family physician, told me early on about *Dr. Susan Love's Breast Book*[16] which became my constant reference and guide. I felt deeply cared for. That did not mean that I was not anxious about the future, especially soon after the diagnosis. I read every article and book I could find about preventing cancer. I nearly bankrupted us buying vitamins and supplements that were recommended and taking a number of assessment tests. Incidentally, the rash which first got

---

[16] Susan M. Love with Karen Lindsey, *Dr. Susan Love's Breast Book*, 5th ed. (Philadelphia: Perseus Books and Da Capo Press, 2010).

everyone's attention was determined not to be part of the cancer symptoms but an unrelated infection.

I would like to add a word about how a serious illness like cancer affects the family of the patient. There is no doubt that family members experience anxiety and exhaustion from the requirements for caregiving and the perceived need to be always upbeat and strong. Yet, care for them is often forgotten in the midst of crisis. This is especially the case for small children or spouses. As an experienced pastoral counselor, my husband knew he had need of a safe place to let down his "burden of optimism" and freely express his feelings, so he sought out a pastoral counselor friend to visit with at regular intervals over the course of my treatments. I would highly recommend that each member of the family or caregiving team be encouraged to seek out a trained professional counselor, pastor, or hospital chaplain to talk with. Such a person knows how to listen and empathize without false cheerfulness or changing the subject. Often, caring friends do not know how to react in a helpful manner to a family's distress. And they are dealing with their own anxiety and love for the patient and family. The American Cancer Society frequently offers support groups for caregivers as well as patients. Children especially need a place and a method of expressing their feelings. In some areas, support groups or summer camps are offered for children of cancer patients. How comforting it is to know that others like you are also going through a hard time and know what it is like. Usually, the Cancer Treatment Center has a counselor on staff available to all family members. Ask about it.

It also helps if the spouse or an adult child can go with the patient to all doctor visits. This provides another set of ears and another brain to process what is being said and to ask questions of the doctors. "Chemo brain" is now a proven phenomenon. It is very normal for a person who has had chemotherapy to experience some degree of memory loss for several months after the treatments. You are not going crazy! Chemotherapy is an assault on all the fast-growing cells of your body, and that includes your brain. Be patient with yourself and allow time, measured in months and years, for full recovery.

And where is God in all this? The Greek term *paraclete*, one who walks alongside, best describes my experience of God's solid presence during this time of challenge and anxiety. I know for certain now that I am not in control of my universe or even in what happens to me or anyone else in the future. "No one is guaranteed tomorrow" has become my guiding principle and surprisingly has eased my anxiety. Thirteen years later, with that in mind, Bob and I are taking the trips we have always wanted to take. I am spending time and money enjoying the four grandchildren who are growing fast and live far enough away that I choose to fly to visit. I am trying to ease my stress on myself: preparing simpler meals and get-togethers and finding many ways to laugh and enjoy life. I still exercise regularly, try to watch my weight, go for regular checkups, and balance my community involvements, my biggest challenge.

And I am trying to live out the scripture that was sent to me on a card before my second surgery: "For surely I know the plans I have for you, says the Lord, plans for your welfare and not for harm, plans to give you a future with hope" (Jer. 29:11 NRSV). Whether that future is long or short, I am making it count for me, for my family, and for my community. This is a lot more certain than the "guarantee" of prevention.

Discovering Life's Meaning via the Shock Waves of Cancer

Charles W. Deweese
Retired Executive Director
Baptist History and Heritage Society

One day in the late summer of 2008, my wife, Mary Jane, and I sat at our kitchen table laughing hilariously at our pathetic health situations. At the moment, we could have laughed or cried—either would have helped. Without any hair or energy, I sat there with a surgically implanted port in the right side of my chest for receiving chemotherapy and a surgically stapled tri-port catheter on the left side of my chest for use in a possible stem cell transplant. I was injecting myself in the abdomen with Neupogen, a drug designed to increase my stem cells so that I could qualify to harvest the cells for a transplant. Sitting next to me, Mary Jane, who had recently had major toe surgery, was infusing herself with an antibiotic drip coming from an IV stand that she had rolled to the table. Our kitchen looked and smelled like a hospital room. Eventually, thank God, both of us recovered from the health issues that led to that laughing moment.

Background, Discovery, and Treatment

Non-Hodgkin's lymphoma transformed my life beginning on 26 July 2007. That day, with pathology report in hand, my oncologist looked me straight in the eyes and confirmed that I had B-cell lymphoma, which he described as being probably large cell (or grade III follicular). This cancer included an abdominal/pelvic mass measuring 15.3 x 10.3 centimeters. Stunned, I listened intently, with Mary Jane sitting beside me, while the doctor described the disease and laid out an immediate and demanding treatment plan. Questions raced through my mind: How could something this large be inside me, attacking my existence, and I not know about it? Where was my future headed? Mary Jane and I left the doctor's office shocked. We had just moved from Tennessee to Georgia. What a start.

In the late fall of 2006, while serving as executive director of the Baptist History and Heritage Society in Brentwood, Tennessee, I had worked out initial arrangements for the Society to move its offices to Mercer University's campus in Atlanta, Georgia, in June 2007. Therefore, in the first half of 2007, Mary Jane and I prepared to make that move.

On February 3, Mary Jane and I signed a purchase and sale agreement for a Georgia builder to construct our new house in Buford. Later that month, we helped Mary Jane's mother move to a nursing unit of her retirement home in Asheville, North Carolina. Then on March 4, my father, also of Asheville, died, following a long battle with diabetes. In late March, we sold our Brentwood, Tennessee, house in which we had lived for more than twenty-five years. We put our furniture in storage and moved into an extended-stay hotel in Brentwood.

In late May, Mary Jane retired from teaching, following a twenty-five-year career in public schools, and we closed on the new house we had built in Buford, Georgia. She moved into our new house the first week in June. I then moved in late on June 14 after coordinating earlier that day the move of Society offices to Atlanta. We thus completed our permanent move to Georgia.

Relieved to have survived all these changes, Mary Jane and I prepared to enjoy our new house, my new workplace, her new retirement opportunities, and our daughter and her family, who lived close by. Although we experienced genuine feelings of loneliness from having extracted ourselves from so many meaningful contexts in Tennessee, we worked hard at being excited about new possibilities. Life looked good.

I have always strongly believed in preventive medicine. In fact, I have had annual physicals throughout my adult life. A few weeks prior to our move to Georgia, I expressed a minor concern to my internist in Nashville about an apparent strange feeling in my abdomen. He manually checked my abdomen and said he thought that I simply had "a tight abdominal muscle"; he completely missed the most important health issue of my life. Then on June 14, while working with the office movers in Atlanta, I discovered a second major sign of my portending health dilemma: I could not keep my belt and pants from slipping throughout the day. Little did I realize until later that my weight loss was a major indicator of trouble that lay ahead.

July 2007 was a big month. Since my wife and I did not know the name or location of a single doctor in Georgia, I relied on the recommendation of our daughter, who also lived in Buford. Thus, on July 13, Mary Jane's birthday, I visited Gwinnett Center Medical Associates in Lawrenceville; they recommended that I see a gastroenterologist, since I had been having trouble with diarrhea. Later that same day, Dr. Sanjay R. Parikh of Atlanta Gastroenterology, also in Lawrenceville, examined me, discovered and questioned a hard spot in my abdomen, recommended both a CAT scan of my abdomen and pelvis and a colonoscopy. On July 17, Dr. Parikh shared with me the report of the CAT scan: "Findings most likely related to lymphoma."

Dr. Parikh arranged for me to have a CAT scan of my chest the very next day and for me to meet with Dr. P. Ravi Sarma, an oncologist in Snellville, Georgia, two days later. With CAT scan reports in hand, Dr. Sarma arranged for me to have a biopsy of the abdominal mass at Gwinnett Medical Center in Lawrenceville on July 23.

On July 26, three days before Mary Jane and I would celebrate our fortieth wedding anniversary, we showed up for my 2:00 p.m. appointment with Dr. Sarma. He confirmed that I had cancer and that the treatment would require chemotherapy. He wrote out four prescriptions and began to make a "staging workup" that included chemotherapy instructions and a bone marrow biopsy on July 31, a PET scan and an echocardiogram on August 1, and the surgical insertion of a port in my chest for receiving chemo drugs on August 3 (that port would stay in place for more than three years, with surgical removal on 16 November 2010).

Dr. Sarma prescribed a chemotherapy regimen called "R-CHOP," which included several drugs. He scheduled my first chemo treatments for August 6–7, to be repeated every two to three weeks for six to eight cycles. I would actually take eight cycles, the last one on 7 January 2008.

Mary Jane and I reported to the chemo administration room at Suburban Hematology-Oncology in Snellville on August 6. For several hours, Rituxan was dripped into me. Then on August 7, three more chemo drugs were administered: Cytoxan, Vincristine, and Adriamycin. On both days and during the following three days, I also took tablet forms of Prednisone. Further, prior to each dripping session, I swallowed the nausea medicine Emend. On August 9, I returned to the office for an injection of Neulasta, designed to help build white blood cells, and was told I would receive such an injection the day after every chemo treatment.

Side effects following the initial August 6–7 treatments were minimal. Those following the August 22 treatment were harsh: a sharp white blood cell decline, extreme fatigue, an intestinal infection, a four-day hospitalization, nausea and vomiting, hair loss, weight loss, and loss of taste. All of this delayed my third treatment by a week. Fatigue became more cumulative every week. Increasingly unable to report to work, I set up a mini-workplace in my home office so that I could do what I could when I felt like it. The fall of 2007 was a tough time.

On 4 February 2008, Dr. Sarma shared with me that I had entered a remission; scans no longer showed evidence of cancerous lymph nodes. However, on 9 June 2008, he told me that the cancer had returned and that a stem cell transplant would be the next best option preceded by a regimen of chemotherapy called RICE: Rituxan, Ifosfamide, Cytoxan, and Etoposide. I received these cancer drugs in two four-day cycles, the first at the end of June and the second during the middle of July. Administration of these treatments took place the first day of each cycle at Surburban Hematology-Oncology and the last three days of each at Gwinnett Medical Center (a three-day hospitalization was required each time because of the dangers of some of the drugs).

Dr. Sarma referred me to Emory Healthcare's Winship Cancer Institute in Atlanta, where Dr. Mary Jo Lechowicz, assistant professor of hematology and oncology, became my physician. Between July 30 and August 5, I had pulmonary tests, an echocardiogram, an EKG, a chest x-ray, a PET scan, a bone marrow biopsy, labs, and a tri-port catheter inserted into the left side of my chest to do the transplant. Then, on August 19, Dr. Lechowicz ruled out more chemo and a stem cell transplant because my most recent PET scan had revealed a sharp decline in the cancer (a major and wonderful surprise). She did recommend that I go ahead and harvest my own stem cells for freezing and possible future use, should cancer return. I took Neupogen injections twice a day for several days to build up my stem cell count, but my body would not produce enough cells to justify harvesting them, so Emory canceled the harvesting. Dr. Lechowicz told me on September 25 that my second remission had set in, and Emory removed the tri-port catheter at the beginning of October. Annual MRIs and labs coordinated by Dr. Lechowicz have continued since 2008; my remission continues into the late fall of 2011.

Chemotherapy treatments in 2007 and 2008 caused harsh side effects. Carefully designed to poison the body just enough to kill cancer, these drugs also attacked healthy parts of my body. The side effects included: hair loss, loss of appetite, cracked lips, mouth sores, a sore throat, digestive and intestinal disorders, extended periods of hiccups, nausea, vomiting, weight loss, dehydration, insomnia, pneumonia, infections, chills, high fevers, dizziness, muscle weakness, numbness and tingling in my fingers and toes, intense ringing in my ears, hearing loss, "metal mouth," "chemo brain," and extreme declines in white blood counts, which resulted in emergency room visits and extended fatigue. Between 2007 and 2011, I received 10 chemo treatments; had 19 CAT scans, PET scans, and MRIs; experienced 6 in-patient hospitalizations (typically for neutropenic fever), including one ambulance experience, and 4 out-patient hospitalizations; had 3 biopsies, 4 echocardiograms, 4 chest x-rays, 19 booster injections for bone marrow cells, 50 labs and blood work, and dozens of visits to my physicians' offices.

Cancer treatment had a big impact on my ability to work. It confined me to my home for months and had a stifling effect on my church and social life, because I was told to avoid contact with people. This was the best means of dealing with low white blood counts that made my immune system highly vulnerable to infection.

So, gratefully, my remission from lymphoma continues. However, my urologist, Dr. Howard C. Goldberg of North Georgia Urology in Lawrenceville, did needle biopsies on my prostate on 28 May 2010 and informed me on June 7 that I had adenocarcinoma, a "low grade" prostate cancer, in one of twelve sections of the prostate. Subsequently, I have had quarterly checkups with him. Still in a "wait and watch" mode, I had another set of biopsies in June 2011. They showed that adenocarcinoma remains in that section and that the Gleason score (a measurement of cancer involvement) had increased from six to seven. Treatment for this will likely get serious. Time will tell.

These opening paragraphs seem pretty matter of fact, and my account may seem needlessly detailed. In truth, nothing about the experiences was matter of fact, and the true story comes out in the unfolding of details. My entire life changed. All of a sudden in 2007, I realized that I had a life-threatening disease. I quickly discovered that the chemotherapy for treating the disease could and would produce a wide array of unwanted effects on my body, mind, soul, and spirit. However, I eventually developed an appreciation for high-powered drugs that could potentially save my life.

At times, I felt that I could handle the treatments by always taking the high road of a positive spirit. At other times, rid of pretensions, I would lie in bed at night and shed tears. Having never suffered a prior major illness in my life, I suddenly found myself on the receiving end of serious medical care.

Honestly, to get thrown against the wall of my finiteness jolted my sense of well-being. I could choose to refuse chemo treatment and die. Or I could choose to get treatment and forge ahead. The unknown would prevail, but support of all kinds from the Lord and his people would help me make sense of the darkness.

Lessons I Learned

My family suffered too. The announcement that I had cancer afflicted my family in many ways. Suddenly, my wife had a sick husband. My married daughters had a sick father. And the decades-long physical stability of this husband and father was at stake. Members of my family cared for me in wonderful ways, but they also suffered alongside me. My wife, daughters, and I shed some tears, but I learned quickly that they would be there for me through every step of the journey.

Mary Jane kept my spirit alive and hopeful. She sat by my side through chemo sessions, drove me hundreds of miles to meet medical needs, fixed meals that I could eat, provided a warm home atmosphere, and took care of all kinds of special needs. She provided constant love and encouragement.

Our daughter, Dana Bowden, who lives with her family in Waco, Texas, performed a marvelous ministry to me for months. Beginning on 29 July 2007, she e-mailed me weekly words of encouragement that were filled with scripture references she had carefully sought out, as well as her pledges to pray for me. I looked forward to Dana's weekly support. In a handwritten note she wrote, "Dad, I'm constantly praying for you! You stay strong and fight this thing! I love you, Dana."

Our daughter, Julie Mobbs, who lives with her family in Buford, Georgia, only five miles from Mary Jane and me, performed special ministries to me as well. On July 26—the day Dr. Sarma confirmed that I had cancer—Julie e-mailed me from her work, "Hi Dad, I Just wanted to let you know that I love you more than you know and that I am praying for you. I know this is a hard day and I have had some heart-to-hearts with God about everything, but no matter what the results of today are we as a family will push forward and get through whatever lies ahead." Later that same day, she drove to our home, and we cried together. Then on August 5, Julie gave to Mary Jane and me a photo album containing thirty-nine photos of family, especially grandchildren; beside each photo, the album included a handwritten verse of a meaningful hymn or spiritual song.

Other members of our family also went out of their way to assist me. Our two sons-in-law put up blinds in our new house, installed ceiling fans, cut my grass, and helped in other practical ways.

I found that along with the loving support of my family, many other sources of healing helped me deal with cancer: the Great Physician; the medical community; powerful drugs; the prayers of the saints; and visits, e-mails, telephone calls, and cards from Christian friends. While dealing with lymphoma treatments in 2007 and 2008, I received more than 350 cards, letters, and e-mails came from churches, Sunday school classes, pastors, deacons, professors, university administrators, Baptist organizational leaders, and friends (I have saved all these written acts of grace). Telephone calls were numerous. Christmas carolers from church sang in our home in December 2007. I owe a huge debt of gratitude to all these sources of healing.

Walter B. Shurden, Baptist historian and friend for decades, e-mailed me: "I try to walk each morning a couple of miles, and I spend some of that time thinking of friends, their joys, and their struggles. You are always on my mind when I am taking that walk."

Duke K. McCall, my former seminary president, sent me a letter that read: "With God all things are possible. So my prayer is that God will guide the doctors and nurses, but add His Divine healing to their efforts."

The most common message I received was the pledge of prayer for Mary Jane and me. John Boyd, long-time friend and pastor of the First Baptist Church of Halifax, Nova Scotia, assured me that his church was "storming heaven" on my behalf.

Pam Durso, associate executive director of the Baptist History and Heritage Society (now executive director of Baptist

Women in Ministry), ministered to me in wonderful ways and assumed additional duties in my absence. I am grateful to her and to Jerry Faught, Mike Williams, and Delane Tew, the Society's board of directors/officers, for their understanding during this challenging time.

Dealing with cancer required lots of patience. The treatment process sometimes seemed agonizingly slow. Coupled with chronic fatigue, the process demanded that I rest constantly. "Be still, and know that I am God!" (Ps 46:10) not only hangs as a framed print in our kitchen; it is also a biblical reality that took on new meaning.

I discovered that engaging in as much productive activity and thought as possible while dealing with cancer, its treatments, and side effects injected meaning into the journey. I dedicated part of my home office to carrying out as many Baptist History and Heritage Society duties as I could. And I read several books in various areas of interest, especially books on lymphoma, since I had a huge learning curve to overcome.

Praying and reading the Bible gave me courage and hope. I prayed often, especially at night while lying in bed. And I re-read the complete New Testament. This reading helped me see that I was not the only person in the world experiencing suffering: Jesus suffered, the apostle Paul suffered, and New Testament Christians at large suffered. Their suffering, on account of their faith, contributed to the viability of my own spiritual life. I graciously received the prayers of the saints, many of whom had walked through deeper waters than I ever had.

The Bible tells me that I (along with everyone else) am created in God's image. My awareness of that biblical truth inserts purpose into the ups and downs of my personal experiences. That is important because I, like all people, never know when the downs will strike or the ups will surge. Through it all, I can know that God loves me and is ever-present.

Receiving wonderful gifts during the treatment process strengthened my spirit. Two such gifts came on 2 July 2008. Between the first and second four-day chemo sessions during treatment for my second cancer, Dana, our daughter in Waco, Texas, gave birth to twins, Lily and Jonathan, meaning that Mary Jane and I then had six grandchildren. I was not able to visit those two grandchildren until late October; however, photos of them prior to the visit enhanced my healing. Then Julie, our daughter in Buford, would give birth to Zoe on 11 February 2010; that seventh grandchild would add joy to the journey.

I found that treatment for cancer is expensive. My private health carrier until I turned 65 plus Medicare and my Medicare supplement plan after that paid more than $300,000 for my care and treatment. (And, if I had had a stem cell transplant, that would have added an additional $400,000–$500,000, which, my insurance company did agree to pay, if necessary.) The amount paid was staggering, but it enabled me to have a future and to maintain health. In the mid-1990s, because my father and grandfather had had cancer, Mary Jane and I had fortunately taken out an AFLAC cancer policy on ourselves, hoping that we would not actually have to use it. That decision significantly helped our personal finances. I learned that keeping good records of medical invoices and insurance payments at times saved us lots of money.

I learned that it is possible to announce prematurely that one is cancer free. I am guilty. Although my oncologist shared with me on 4 February 2008 that I was in remission following my initial eight rounds of chemotherapy, I interpreted that to mean more than it did. During the spring of 2008, things seemed to go well. During the Society's annual meeting in Atlanta on May 22–24, I projected the image of someone headed toward total healing, and I honestly felt that complete healing was happening. But I learned on June 9 that the cancer had returned. Looking in the mirror after losing my hair the second time helped me know that I had made a mistake in declaring myself well.

I realized that all healing is temporary. Physical death will come. Perhaps the deaths of my father on 4 March 2007 and of my mother-in-law on 2 January 2008 reinforced that for me. Admittedly, I am not eager for that to happen to me anytime soon. But it will come. So, I now live with some challenging questions: Will I commit myself to Christ's Lordship in every facet and phase of my life? Will I invest my gifts, time, and financial resources in things that matter?

Hope drives the mystery of cancer. My urologist will continue to monitor my prostate cancer, and my oncologists will continue to check on my remission from lymphoma. What will the future hold? Who knows? Whatever happens, I have decided that my task is to do the best I can with the health I have. I thank God for retirement, for opportunities, for caring people, for family, and for life. Regardless of my circumstances, I claim hope from the Lord of history who promises to be with me always.

Life's Fragility and God's Sufficiency

Cindy McClain
Marketing Product Manager with FamilyLife,
A Ministry of Cru International
(Formerly Campus Crusade for Christ International)
Member of Saddle Creek Church, Little Rock, Arkansas

I returned home from work to find my furniture had been rearranged. The arrangement was random—sofas against doors, bureaus separated from matching mirrors, chairs facing walls. As I walked through the house, I caught a glimpse of a figure fleeing through the back door, and I hurried to catch up with him. Puzzled, I cried out, "Why are you doing this?" but I didn't get an answer. By then the figure was out of sight.

I woke drenched in sweat. For a minute I was disoriented, and then I realized I had been dreaming. My hand moved to my chest, now covered in bandages. I remembered I had undergone surgery. I was now a breast cancer survivor.

This intruder invaded my sleep a few days after I was discharged from Vanderbilt University Hospital. So vivid was the dream, I can still see the images in my mind. What is it like to have cancer? It's having your life rearranged without order or meaning. It's a total loss of control.

Despite a history of fibrocystic breasts, I never imagined I would develop breast cancer. After all, the only family history I knew was my maternal grandfather who had a cancerous lump removed from his chest around age seventy and lived, without further treatment, to age ninety, when he died of a stroke. By the time I reached forty, I had had so many cysts that I had lost count. I had even become flippant when finding a new one.

So, when I felt yet another cyst in spring 2003, I was not concerned. It was smooth, round, and rubbery, all the marks of a cyst. My yearly mammogram was scheduled for April, and when I went in for it, the breast surgeon confirmed it was a cyst. Just to be sure, he ordered an ultrasound, and sure enough, the round, rubbery object was a cyst.

In past years, my doctors had drained cysts using a syringe, but by now the prevailing practice was to leave them alone unless they became painful, because chances were they would just refill. So I left the clinic that day with my cyst intact and with no more thought about it.

My job as a marketing strategist with LifeWay Christian Resources in Nashville kept me busy. One of my assignments was to plan and coordinate LifeWay's exhibit at the annual Southern Baptist Convention meeting in Phoenix that year, and by April we were fully immersed in those plans. It wasn't until July, after the Convention was over, that I noticed the cyst was larger and had changed texture. Now it was hard and elongated, not round and rubbery. But I kept reassuring myself it was just a cyst. After all, the ultrasound had confirmed it.

By October the cyst was larger and painful to touch. I decided to call the Vanderbilt Breast Center and ask for an appointment to get it drained. The Center scheduled me in quickly. Within a week, on Thursday, October 30, I was lying on the table, the trusty ultrasound machine whirring softly beside me. The radiologist had performed this procedure on me so many times we were practically on a first-name basis.

He squirted the lubricating gel and began moving the ultrasound wand around the breast. I twisted my head and tried to see the screen. I had viewed many cysts on the screen before, so I sort of knew what to look for. But this time I couldn't see the screen. I heard the radiologist say quietly, "We need to do a core biopsy." The nurse assisting him turned and reached for different equipment. The room suddenly became quiet.

In that moment, I knew. I knew it wasn't just another cyst. This time there wouldn't be a syringe full of brownish-greenish fluid and jokes about how big it was. This time there would be a different diagnosis, and life as I had known it would change.

Cancer treatment can consume one's life, especially if the tumor is considered at least locally advanced. Once the diagnosis is made, more tests are done to determine its "stage" (a rating of 0 to 4, with 0 being pre-cancerous and 4 being metastatic disease) as well as determining factors such the tumor's hormone receptivity (positive or negative), the presence or absence of the Her2 protein, and the rate of cell division. All these factors are considered in the course of treatment options presented to a patient. Then there are additional tests to determine if the patient's body can withstand treatment. (Some chemotherapy drugs as well as radiation can damage the heart and other organs.)

Since my tumor was determined to be locally advanced and my diagnosis occurred at what is considered a young age (forties), all three treatment options—surgery, chemotherapy, and radiation—were recommended. I had to choose a surgeon, oncologist, and radiologist. I had to decide if I wanted to start with surgery immediately or take chemotherapy first to shrink the tumor.

In the days following my diagnosis, I felt like I had been hit by a tsunami. I was swept into a steady stream of medical appointments and tests. I became consumed with keeping up with them, sorting through information and recommendations, and making decisions. Being single, I didn't have a spouse upon whom to lean, so my emotions had to be pushed aside in order for me to think through the information given and make decisions. Well-meaning friends referred me to relatives or acquaintances who were breast cancer survivors, but I quickly learned conversations with them weren't always helpful. Learning about one woman's experience with stage 1 hormone-positive breast cancer is entirely different from learning about another's stage 3 hormone-negative breast cancer. Cancer is not the same in every patient; it is actually a very individualistic disease, and every person's treatment plan is unique within recommended standards agreed upon in the medical community.

Breast cancer is usually a slow-growing cancer, and a woman can take a few weeks to consider treatment options. Because my tumor's growth rate was aggressive, I didn't have a lot of time to consider options. I also learned that navigating the specialized medical world can be overwhelming. Consider the decisions of choosing a surgeon, oncologist, and radiologist. My life would be in their hands. How should I choose them? I decided to trust the surgeon at the Vanderbilt Breast Center in Tennessee to whom I was assigned, Dr. Mark Kelley, and he turned out to be a godsend. When appointments for needed tests weren't available as soon as desired, he or his staff convinced clinics to work me in. When the oncologist he recommended didn't have an opening for a new patient until three weeks later, he asked her to see me sooner. The course of treatment recommended to me involved starting with chemotherapy, and within three weeks of my diagnosis I was sitting in the infusion center with two friends watching Taxol, my first chemotherapy drug, drip into the newly installed port. To accomplish so much in just three weeks was a miracle.

My course of treatment lasted nine months and involved three different chemotherapy drugs, radiation, and surgery. It was grueling, but I was able to work full-time all but three of those months, and even during those three months I was able to work part-time. The hardest phase of treatment was chemotherapy, especially the drugs Adriamycin and Cytoxan. Adriamycin and Cytoxan (known as A/C) are among the granddaddies of cancer drugs. Developed more than fifty years ago, they act like Agent Orange, killing good cells and bad cells. Side effects can include severe anemia, weakened immune systems, and debilitating nausea. More recently developed drugs, like Taxol, have fewer side effects and are tolerated much better. However, reactions to drugs are very individualized. While I had significant difficulties with Adriamycin and Cytoxan and very few with Taxol, I know women for whom the opposite was true.

An unexpected difficulty I encountered was temporary paralysis of my arm following surgery. An uncommon complication of a mastectomy is paralysis resulting from pressure during the surgery on the brachial nerve that runs from the spine, through the armpit area, and down the arm. In my case the paralysis was temporary, lasting about three months, although I still have some tingling in my thumb, index finger, and middle finger.

Another complication I experienced was neutropenia, a condition where the white blood cell count drops too low and the immune system becomes too weak to fight off even the simplest infection. I became neutropenic just before my last chemo treatment. My white blood cell count plummeted to 0.4; normal range is between 4 and 10. I had sores in my mouth, a side effect of chemotherapy, and a normally harmless bacteria found in my mouth entered my bloodstream where it set up an infection. The condition resulted in a five-day hospital stay, two pints of blood, and four weeks of intravenous antibiotics.

I am now going on eight years as a cancer survivor without sign of a recurrence. The odds of my having cancer again have dropped back to the percentage for any American woman. After I passed the five-year mark, I breathed easier. Still, a day doesn't go by without my thinking about it, mostly because I can't get dressed without seeing the physical reminders.

The emotional and spiritual marks remain as well. While I have not let cancer define me, it is never far from my mind. I learned that life is fragile; it can turn on a dime. We are not promised length of days on earth or freedom from suffering. Rather, we are promised God's presence in times of trouble (Isaiah 43:2). When life has overwhelmed us, he tells us he knows the path ahead (Psalm 142:3). We are promised a home with him one day (John 6:54).

If we believe in the sovereignty of God, then that belief must prevail through the good and the bad. God cannot be sovereign over the good things that happen to us but not the bad. This concept can be difficult to fathom, because it requires us to face the fact God allows bad things to happen.

Job learned it. So did Joseph. So did Peter and Paul and many others. But they also learned that when God allows bad things to happen, it is for a purpose, and over time we may or may not come to understand that purpose. That's where faith must prevail. Paul wrote, "I have been crucified with Christ; and it is no longer I who live, but Christ lives in me; and the life which I now live in the flesh I live by faith in the Son of God, who loved me and gave Himself up for me" (Gal. 2:20 NASB).

In facing cancer, I had to examine my belief in God's sovereignty as well. While it is true that cancer is caused by flawed cell division that goes unchecked by the body's immune system, I had to accept the fact that flawed cell division happens constantly in our bodies, and in the vast majority of people, their immune systems destroy the flawed cells. In my body, however, the flawed cell division kept going; my immune system couldn't stop it. And the larger truth was that God allowed the flawed cell division to continue.

But God is also always sufficient, and he proved his sufficiency to me in a myriad of ways during those nine months of treatment. Embracing his sovereignty also strengthened my belief in his sufficiency. While I would never want to go through the cancer treatments again, I am grateful for what I learned through the experience—about God, about his grace and love, and about my faith in him. I am also grateful for the relationships that were forged with neighbors, coworkers, and fellow church members and the love they showered on me. They were the hands and feet of Jesus.

If I try to include everyone who walked with me through cancer, I'll surely forget some, but I want to list a few key persons:

Mother: Eighty-three at the time, my mother stayed with me for seven months. She fixed food and made me eat when I didn't feel like it. She washed clothes and fixed meals and did the day-to-day housework. She sat with me when the nausea was overwhelming and took my temperature when I felt too warm. She fussed over me continually. You're never too old to need your mother, and when I needed mine, she was there.

Dottie: My neighbor Dottie became my cancer mentor. Until my diagnosis, my contacts with Dot and Perry had been casual greetings as we encountered one another coming or going. A week or so after my diagnosis, Dottie stopped by. She had noticed a number of cars stopping by my home and wanted to know if something was wrong. "I have breast cancer, Dot," I said, choking on the words. "Well, so do I!" she exclaimed. Unbeknownst to me, Dottie had been treated four years earlier for locally advanced breast cancer and was now in stage 4 with a metastasis in her liver. But she didn't let her diagnosis get her down. She brought homemade chicken noodle soup and reassured my mother when I felt sick as a dog. When my temperature rose too high, she drove us to the emergency room and stayed with us until my discharge at midnight. When it was time for me to be fitted for a mastectomy bra, she drove me to the shop she used and helped me choose. A woman of faith, she showed me how one lives with cancer—and dies in peace knowing her life was in God's hands. One of my favorite memories of Dot is catching a glimpse of her with Perry one day as they left for a wedding. Tanned from a beach vacation, she wore a slim black skirt, black and white print shell, and heeled sandals. She looked fabulous. Only a few of us knew she was bald under that wig and had tumors in her liver that weren't responding to treatment. But she was as spunky as ever. Cancer didn't defeat her.

Donna, Missey, and Miriam: My three friends from the LifeWay marketing department became my caregiver angels, coordinating meals, housecleaning, and transportation with people at work and church; sitting with me through chemo treatments; and performing countless other acts of kindness. I can never repay them for everything they did.

Grace Community Church: The members of Grace brought new meaning to the word ministry. Everyone was incredibly giving: housecleaning, meals, transportation, visits. I cannot imagine how others get through cancer without a faith family.

Two years after I finished treatment, I came across an online article written by John Piper after he was diagnosed with prostate cancer. Titled "Don't Waste Your Cancer," Piper gave ten thoughts to consider with a cancer diagnosis. I keep this article in my journal and pull it out every so often to read again. It reminds me that in God's sovereignty there is a purpose for everything—even the things we can't understand:

You will waste your cancer if you do not believe it is designed for you by God.

You will waste your cancer if you believe it is a curse and
   not a gift.
You will waste your cancer if you seek comfort from your
   odds rather than from God.
You will waste your cancer if you refuse to think about
   death.
You will waste your cancer if you think that "beating"
   cancer means staying alive rather than cherishing Christ.
You will waste your cancer if you spend too much time
   reading about cancer and not enough time reading
   about God.
You will waste your cancer if you let it drive you into
   solitude instead of deepen your relationships with
   manifest affection.
You will waste your cancer if you grieve as those who have
   no hope.
You will waste your cancer if you treat sin as casually as
   before.
You will waste your cancer if you fail to use it as a means of
   witness to the truth and glory of Christ.[17]

If I spend time trying to figure out why God allowed me to
have cancer instead of what I can learn from it or do as a result, I
will have wasted the experience.

God used cancer to create within me a longing for his
kingdom. Romans, chapter 8 says, "I consider that the sufferings
of this present time are not worth comparing with the glory
about to be revealed to us. For the creation waits with eager
longing for the revealing of the children of God" (vv. 18–19
NRSV). The only thing that really matters in this world is your

---

[17] John Piper, "First Person: Don't waste your cancer," 6 April
2006, http:// www.bpnews.net.

relationship with him. He is truly sufficient. He met my every need, oftentimes through the ministry of others. The things of this earth really are temporary; only God's kingdom will last.

God, Me, and Cancer

Gerald L. Durley
Pastor
Providence Missionary Baptist Church
Atlanta, Georgia

It was a beautiful, clear, rather crisp Monday morning when the doctor's office called and asked me to come in on Thursday for a consultation. I, of course, was pleased to have finally heard from him since I had been advised to take a colonoscopy. The intriguing part of my taking the colonoscopy was that for years I had served as the director of the Health Promotion Resource Center at the Morehouse School of Medicine in Atlanta, Georgia. In that capacity, my primary responsibilities were to promote healthy awareness and disease prevention, and to raise the level of awareness among people as to potential health concerns that they may encounter. Diet, exercise, and most certainly taking the appropriate health examinations at suggested times were of prime importance.

When a friend casually asked if I had ever taken a colonoscopy, I chuckled and said, "My job is to advise people about taking care of themselves." I politely let his concern for my well-being pass, but I honestly asked myself what could it hurt since I had not had the examination. When one is so deeply involved in his or her profession, whatever it may be, one may tend to overlook or disregard advice shared with others. I realize now that I was a premier violator of this fact. I called for an appointment and lackadaisically went for my examination. After all, I had no symptoms of illness or pain; therefore, I had no fear of the results of a routine procedure.

Being a Christian minister for the past thirty-five years only reinforced my belief that everything was fine and this procedure was merely a time-consuming motion. I believed that anything that I had to encounter would be overcome by my unyielding, uncompromising faith in God. I felt that I could not lose, because if the results came back negative, I would thank, and even praise God. If they returned positive, I knew that God could heal any condition. During my life, if I ever felt or thought that I had to face an impossible situation, I undoubtedly knew that my faith would turn impossibilities into possibilities!

With the utmost confidence and patience, I listened as the doctor said, "The results for your examination are inconclusive, and, therefore, I feel that to be more definitive in my diagnosis a few more tests will be required." Those words penetrated, momentarily, my impenetrable faith. I instantly wondered what a minister, who has lived the majority of his life facing and overcoming seemingly insurmountable odds, does when those unexpectedly frightening words are spoken so matter-of-factly. My initial reaction was, "Is he talking to me about my test results?" Instantly, I felt and said under my breath, "That's impossible." I immediately questioned the words "a few more tests will be required." I wondered why. There must have been a misinterpretation of the data, because my test results should not indicate polyps that might be cancerous. That's impossible. I am the person charged with informing others about preventive health care; plus I also pray for the wellness and healing of others.

More tests—even the thought of subjecting myself to an MRI, a CAT scan, or ultrasound seemed unimaginable, if not, threatening. I thought to myself, "I can't believe this. I've never even been in the hospital for any length of time." Immediately I responded, as do many who face this new challenge, "Anything—but CANCER. Not the BIG C." I have so much to live for and so many things to accomplish.

To fully appreciate why I had the unmitigated gall to think and then shout, "That's impossible," it is necessary to understand who I am and what has compelled me to face, challenge, and conquer seemingly overwhelming circumstances. I was born into a family whose father abruptly abandoned the field of entertainment and became a powerful preacher of the gospel. He one day, seemingly for no reason, changed his lifestyle and demanded that everyone associated with him should do the same. There were children in our family when my father convicted, converted, convinced, and committed to the notion that "nothing is impossible for God." He literally believed and practiced that if he had faith in God, then nothing would be impossible (Mt 17:20). Thirteen years later, a set of twins and new daughter increased our family to eight. He believed and drilled that whatever catastrophe we may face throughout life, nothing was impossible for God, and that God would guide us safely through. My father constantly told our family that with men and women things may appear impossible, but with God all things are possible (Mt 19:26). These words formed the core of what I believed then, and I am more certain of them today. I continue to use the words of my father to confront any and all calamities that seek to derail me from accomplishing my goals for life.

To comprehend the depth of my belief that nothing is impossible for God, I used it to overcome a severe stuttering problem that kept me back in school. This same focused belief system enabled me to become intensely involved in the early days of the civil rights movement while completing college. Graduating from college and being asked to be a member of the first group of US Peace Corps Volunteers who were sent to serve in Nigeria, I was startled, and my belief that anything is possible was reinforced. I wondered how they could select me as a volunteer since my involvement with the civil rights movement was so intense. Leaving Nigeria, I was recruited to play for the All National Basketball Team of Switzerland. Once again, I sensed God's hands manipulating my young life. I then returned to America and completed a master's degree and a doctorate in psychology. By this time, I was convinced there was a guiding force governing my life. I had never planned to be on a national basketball team or go on to two graduate schools. I accepted the fact that all of this was possible because of my belief that nothing is impossible for God—yet I continued to feel that the news of me having cancer just wasn't possible. I had lived and played by the rules but was now facing CANCER.

Like most who believe and trust God, I knew and quoted familiar clichés when faced with seemingly impossible situations. At one time or another, we have all utilized these verbal tidbits to shore up our belief system and thereby be assured of success. I have used these and other quotes when life's circumstances appeared impossible:

"There is no failure in God."
"God will never give you more than you can bear."
"God is able to subdue all things."
"Nothing is too big for God."

However, I have experienced that when one is finally confronted with the possibility of having cancer, fear invades one's entire thoughts and belief system, and such fear negatively challenges all of those well-meaning words of faith.

On that fateful morning, all I heard was, "We need to conduct more tests to determine whether the initial findings, of cancerous polyps, are valid." My thoughts forced me to imagine being squeezed into, and confined within, the "casket" of the

MRI machine. I felt that I could not do it. It would be impossible. I was deeply afraid of having an MRI, but a friend of mine located an open MRI machine, and the fear that I felt was impossible became possible. When I completed all of the requested examinations, I was informed that I had colon cancer. My immediate response, upon accepting the diagnosis, was that God would not abandon me. I honestly believed that this was a misdiagnosis. I reasoned that as much as I had depended on God, as many pat phrases that I knew, as many sermons that I had preached, as many people that I had comforted, that news was simply impossible. My mind was challenged by this new reality. This sweeping mental and spiritual tug of war reminded me that no one is exempt from having his or her faith tested.

What surprised me at the doctor's final, official pronouncement of my health condition was that what I initially thought was impossible was now more than possible. It was a fact; I had cancer. All of the statements for rationalizing why this could not be possible immediately captured and flooded my very being. I eat right and exercise regularly, and I am a faithful husband, a good father, and a Christian minister—all of that exploded in my head. I was shocked. When cancer was mentioned, it ignited a spiritual transformation that forced me to seek my frequently quoted spiritual clichés, proven scriptures, and prayers and cling to them to survive. Now I had to face the medical truth that I had cancer, and I had to believe that nothing is impossible with God, even though I confusedly shouted, "That's impossible."

For me to accept this news was a real challenge, and I questioned my readiness to move forward positively. I envisioned and created in my mind what was a death sentence. I had heard that one goes through chemotherapy treatments for a period, filled with tiredness and multiple side effects and then ultimately death. How could God allow this to happen? It just seemed impossible. The dreaded dooming effect of doubt began to consume my thoughts. I secretly questioned whether God would take what I thought was an impossible medical finding and cure me? Maybe for the first time, I honestly sought God's counsel, comfort, and guidance. From that moment on, my faith in God's ability to honor his healing promises and my acceptance that the doctors knew more than I did changed my entire outlook and expectations for the future.

Laparoscopic surgery was performed, and the diseased section of the colon was removed. What I feared was impossible—my acquiring the disease and then being cured—became possible. I can attest now, more than ever before, that when biblical words that encourage us to trust in God become an integral part of our belief system and moments of crisis occur, facing the truth is the first step in testing our faith and belief system. I have never doubted or questioned whether God had the omnipotent power to cure me; however, I did question whether it was his will to do it. I rationalized that his will and my desire might not be in harmony. I immediately remembered the verse, "By his stripes we are healed." What does that really mean? It means that no weapon (i.e., cancer) formed against me can win. I needed the same words of wisdom to encourage me to keep my faith.

Deep down inside, I could not shake the feeling that my undesired medical report was impossible. I had played by the rules, obeyed God's directives, and treated neighbors and foes with dignity, so how could God permit cancer to inhabit my body? These damaged feelings of God's unfaithfulness brought on tinges of disappointment, frustration, and maybe even a little anger. In the midst of these extremely compelling emotions to surrender to God, I reached back and recalled another cliché, "Let this cup pass from me." I asked myself why I should be excluded from this medical cup of cancer. I found my comfort and peace when I remembered and confided in the words,

"Father, into your hands I surrender my spirit, will, and future. Have your way with me." When these words became a reality in my spirit, I finally secured a sense of absolute peace.

I was overpowered and engulfed in an atmosphere that surrounded me with an assurance that everything was in divine order. This inner peace allowed me to accept my condition, and the familiar clichés now had new meaning. I began this new, exciting journey with optimistic fervor. The laparoscopic surgery was successful. We all celebrated until I was confronted with the news that a preventive procedure—ten months of chemo-therapy—was recommended. My first reaction was that the operation was not as successful as I had been led to believe. Hence, chemotherapy would be required. Just for a fleeting moment, feelings of acute anxiety controlled my emotions. They were short-lived. I now was forced to believe that nothing was impossible for God, even curing my cancer.

I was instructed to take chemotherapy every Monday. I knew that such treatments were in the best interest of my long-term health, and I reluctantly joined my new chemotherapy family in our assigned chairs. I quickly realized that the time required for the treatments limited my normally extremely busy schedule. I realize now that God has an uncanny way of using his time to create new vistas of understanding through fellowship and love. I was introduced to those who sat next to me during our treatments. I ignorantly surmised that those who knew me might have been questioning my faith in God since they saw me as sick as they were. This was faulty thinking on my part. Soon my chemotherapy family began to pray with, and for, each other, and a mutual admiration support society was born. We shared stories of fear, doubt, joy, laughter, losses, victories, tears, pain, and hope. Each personal revelation was a source of strength for each of us. Soon, the clinicians became a part of our support family, and a true healing environment was created, whether we had cancer or not.

A lesson was reinforced for me, which I will forever cherish: God uses other people to bring blessings into our lives. We must be open and willing to receive whomever God sends into our lives by removing our doubts, fears, and feelings of hopelessness. I now acknowledge the fact that, even though I am a person of faith and a pastor, I do not have to be the end all for everyone—I am human too!

Eventually, the smell of the medicine during the chemotherapy, which occasionally upset my stomach, became a fragrance of love, support, companionship, and genuine caring. I smiled each week and entered the clinic in anticipation to see how God would unfold positive possibilities during our treatment time together. The cleaning of the port, waiting for the blood count, and the injection of the medicine all became a meaningful part of God's divine plan for my life. Chemotherapy did not become any easier, nor did I look forward to it, but each treatment increased my faith in God.

The fears and apprehensions that I experienced when I was informed that I had colon cancer remained until I began to believe that God really could do what he promised. Accepting that reality restored my inner peace. I came to a healthy level of understanding with God about cancer.

I now accept the fact that regardless of the catastrophic news that we may receive, no one is exempt from the abrupt changes of life. What is important is our response to what may appear, at the time, life-threatening or ending. To respond, "That's impossible," is a little naïve because anything can happen to any of us at anytime.

Events and circumstances do not happen because we are good, bad, indifferent, rich, poor or even in the wrong place. It is paramount to remember that rather than allowing those destructive feelings of "Why me? What did I do to deserve this?" to take charge, we must realize that God is ultimately in charge and will render the final results. Know and believe that nothing is impossible for God and that what may appear to be disastrous may actually turn into a period of divine spiritual, personal growth.

When a situation seems impossible and the answers to our questions leave us full of doubt and the words "Nothing is impossible with God" have lost their significance, it's time to stop and refocus our thoughts. I finally found my peace and assurance when I heard the words, "When cancer returns, it comes with a vengeance"; I rejected those words immediately. I knew that the return of cancer was possible. Those words now were muffled because I knew that since God healed me once, he could and would do it again.

What these spiritually enriching and empowering months have meant for me personally is that I have become a much more understanding and accepting-of-life human being. My appreciation of what can unexpectedly transpire in anyone's life, to alter his or her course of life, has been enhanced. When I, or anyone, is forced to face the fact that cancer has become a resident in our body, it does not necessarily mean that it is a permanent resident. Tragedy is a visitor in all of our lives, and there are lessons to be learned during these unique times. I learned that once cancer has been diagnosed, it should not be an all-consuming way of life. Cancer is merely a comma in the sentence of life and not necessarily a period.

I want to report to anyone reading these words and thoughts of inspiration, comfort, and hopefully guidance that having shared the last two years with cancer, I am a better pastor. The fear of, and acceptance of, the fact that I had cancer has greatly improved my prayer life. This journey has opened up my mind and spirit to broader new visions for service.

Family, friends, and church members are cherished even more. I view from an entirely different perspective those whom I did not understand or who did not understand or appreciate my positions.

When one properly prepares to travel the long and winding road of cancer, it can be life enriching and filled with unimagined, great possibilities. Cancer, when put in its appropriate context, will teach that there is a lesson to be learned about living if it is accepted that "Nothing is impossible for God." What we may see as impossible for whatever reason, God has an answer.

When you or a loved one is told that cancer has been discovered in your body, rather than say, as I did, "That's impossible!" regard it as yet another opportunity to remember that nothing is impossible for God.

Allowing Space for Grace

Juno M. Sharp
Retired Social Worker
Member, Dawson Memorial Baptist Church,
Homewood, Alabama

The year before I was diagnosed with breast cancer, my father died at age ninety-one. In an article written several months after he died, I expressed a few thoughts on how my family's Christian faith and beliefs had helped us cope with the "long goodbye" of a patient with Alzheimer's disease. I titled the essay, "Staying a Step Behind Grace." I believe that when we seek God and believe that he is there along life's journey, we can act with a little less panic and urgency, and with a little more humility and gratefulness. A year later, after experiencing my father's death and after writing and reading about grace, my own words would both challenge and encourage me.

For me, the concept of grace can move from a reassuring spiritual belief into a practical reality. By not rushing forward, we allow space for acts of grace to pave the path before us. We can more readily recognize acts of kindness as expressions of grace sent by a loving Father who wants to bless us in difficult times. An attitude of acceptance and gratitude is formed. We can see those mercies fill the spaces with God's grace in troubled times through days of tears and laughter, frustrations, and sweet surprises.

Philip Yancey's inspirational book, *What's So Amazing About Grace?*, illuminates varied aspects of God's grace. Within the framework of my Christian beliefs, the book reminds us that God grants grace to those who trust in him and that such grace is sufficient. My eyes and heart just need to recognize and receive it without demanding, hurrying, or worrying. Discernment is needed in knowing when to act on instincts and knowledge and when to wait.

In October 1999, I discovered a lump in my breast that required immediate attention. After the lump in my throat and the knot in my stomach eased, my husband and I knew that the first thing to do was pray to the Lord for direction and peace of mind. Whether I prayed for healing that night, I truly do not remember. I must have, but my clearest impression was the realization that if I took stock of my situation, everything needed for healing and encouragement was already available to me. It was encouraging to know that I did not suddenly need to formulate a belief system, or search for a social support network, or wish for a loving family, or scramble for medical experts. All were at hand. Having never experienced any health crises, I was now in one requiring a sincere trust.

As a Christian by the grace of my Lord and Savior, Jesus Christ, and possessing a lifelong grounding in beliefs of the Southern Baptist persuasion, my faith was real to me. As a hospice volunteer for years, then a social worker on a hospital geriatric unit, my awareness of the potential for death and dying was realistic. Perhaps because of this background, no time was spent musing about "Why Me?" Rather, "Why not me?" is the operative attitude when bad things, when bad luck, disease, accidents, foolishness, or violence happen. The rain truly falls on the just and the unjust. Both godless and pious persons seek help in emergency rooms and oncologists' offices daily. Persons with positive attitudes and downbeat cynics with despairing, negative thoughts journey down the same hospital hallways, and neither attitude is a determinant nor predictor for a healing of disease, according to all medical research, although we would love to believe otherwise. What belief and attitude bring to the equation is the more crucial element not in how one dies, but rather in how one chooses to live until she says goodbye.

A physician-friend who is widely read and wise shared a passage with me from *Moby-Dick* by Herman Melville, in which the author describes the intricate manner in which the yards and yards of roping of the harpoon lines are coiled and twisted about the oarsmen sitting in rows in the little boats sent out from the mother whale-ship when a whale is sighted. They are so expert and so accustomed to the serpentine lines about them that the terrific risks and terrors of the sea over time have become lost to them. It is only when an arm or leg becomes caught up in the roping as a harpoon is launched that the peril in which they literally sit is realized as an oarsman is lost at sea and drowned. All the while, everything seems so calm and normal. Melville expands the theme, "But why say more? All men live enveloped in whale lines. All are born with halters round their necks; but it is only when caught in the swift, sudden turn of death, that mortals realize the silent, subtle, ever-present perils of life. And if you be a philosopher, though seated in the whale-boat, you would not at heart feel one whit more of terror, than though seated before your evening fire with a poker, and not a harpoon, by your side."[18] This is a stunning reminder that to live is to be at risk. Man is born to die.

My dear Aunt Nelle told me before her death from lung cancer, "Juno, everybody is going to have something." It was her way of voicing the inevitability of death and of saying that she accepted her illness and preferred to have a disease that did not rob her of her mind as Alzheimer's disease had robbed her brother and my father.

---

[18] Herman Melville, *Moby-Dick or, The Whale* (New York: Penguin Putnam, 1998) 274.

I immediately contacted several close friends who had been treated for breast cancer and were a source of specific knowledge and wisdom. They freely shared experiences, treatments, and opinions, but none was dogmatic with "should dos and must dos." All were encouraging and insightful. It did not take long to select the doctors whom I would contact at the hospital where I worked. While walking to the gynecologist's office, I had a clear image that I was stepping on a moving sidewalk, and that there would be no getting off for a while. After choosing my doctors, there would be little else for me to do but listen, ask questions to understand, and follow their advice. That also involved trust.

After the surgeon examined all the pathology reports, he "gave us the bad news in the nicest possible way," according to my husband. He was that rare surgeon who has a pleasant bedside manner, not especially cautious in sharing a wry sense of humor, and a favorite of all the operating room nurses. We were both immediately at ease with him. We knew he was an excellent surgeon, but his pleasing personality was a comfort during an anxious time.

Physicians speak in scientific terms, percentages, and facts, because they are not prophets. There are too many unknowns and variables in each human condition that impact recovery. This may seem cold, but cautious optimism and realistic expectations are a better course.

I often recall a sermon given by the late John Claypool, of St. Luke's Episcopal Church in Mountain Brook, Alabama, entitled, "It's Simply to Early to Tell." He used an ancient Chinese parable to illustrate the value of a balanced perspective, rather than becoming overly optimistic over a stroke of good luck or filled with gloom and doom about a bit of bad luck or unhappy news. When an old Chinese peasant found a few coins, his friends were jubilant about the find, but the old man said, "It is simply too early to tell." Later, the money caused discord in his family. When the man's son broke his leg falling off a horse, the man said, "It is simply to early to tell." Later, the injury spared his son being drafted into the army and certain death. The point was that we do not know the future or God's complete plans for us, or how God's redemptive love will be worked out in our lives. In facing a medical crisis, it is so helpful to have a balanced perspective. Realistic expectations are formed when we balance the medical facts of the diagnosis, treatment options, our personality, our coping strategies, and our support systems of friends, family, and faith.

Within a week of discovery, I had seen a gynecologist and a surgeon, who after a biopsy and lumpectomy, with clear margins, steered me toward physicians for radiation and oncology assessments. Because of my age, the size, type, antigen, and estrogen receptivity of the tumor, a course of chemotherapy followed by a series of radiation treatments was advised and scheduled. The oncologist advised me that because, at age fifty, I was on the cusp of menopause, chemotherapy would propel me right into it. Great, something else to look forward to. Later, I would wonder which side effects to attribute to which condition.

Now that I had a clear diagnosis and treatment plan, it was time to really prepare myself for the long haul. I had another one of those clear, compelling thoughts that it was time to rally all the friends who had expressed concern and who stood by in a crisis to do something. I phoned our associate pastor, who is a man of prayer and sensitivity, and asked him to conduct a prayer service where friends could unite for prayer, hymns, and scripture, and to commit this journey of treatment to the Lord. One friend provided her home; another brought oil for anointing and searched for special scriptures to read. Sixteen of us gathered that night of November 18. We heard readings from Psalm 30 on the blessings of answered prayer and from James

5:13-16, and the names of Jehovah were recounted. We heard that the meanings of "salvation" in the Greek include rescue, deliverance, and preservation.

It was a humbling experience to give myself over to the unknown, all the while praying for healing, exposing any weakness or frailties of faith and spirit, while yearning for more of Christ in me. It was a precious and loving time, one to cherish and remember not just for the days of chemotherapy and radiation that lay ahead, but forever. The fellowship of believers, of the faithful, of those who pray in one accord, is a bonding, soul-lifting, precious encouragement to all.

One thing that I learned from other cancer survivors is that one's life goes on, whether one has cancer or not, and a person must schedule and plan for little things to look forward to all along the way. With this in mind, my daughter and son-in-law planned a special trip for New Year's Eve celebration of the Millennium in January 2000 to a "warm place in South Florida." So my first chemotherapy treatment was timed to allow for that trip. I also continued to work my three-day-a-week schedule at the hospital with the support of an understanding supervisor and friends on the staff. They were wonderful and picked up the slack for me from time to time. It was good to have a schedule and something that made me get up and get going or keep going. Fortunately, our insurance coverage covered my medical care. This spared us the worry of financial ruin, which many individuals face.

My friends often reminded me (lest I forget) that my husband was extremely supportive. With his faith, his steady hand, his humor, his innate kindness, he kept me going. He created distractions and cooked when I could not tell the difference between steak and cardboard. (Yes, some chemotherapy drugs do cause "metal mouth.") That is not a description of his cooking. When I was worried about a home repair needing attention, he handled it and spared me the details. He understood that if I was crying in a bubble bath and had aches and weakness, I would get over it and the sob session was just part of my coping, not despairing. He knew when to hover and when to leave me alone.

It was important to allow friends to help in their own way. Not everyone can do everything. One friend, a banker, mailed a hand-written note every week, written during his prayer time. His verses for me were often from Jeremiah. I love Jeremiah 17:14 (NRSV): "Heal me, O Lord, and I shall be healed; save me and I shall be saved; for you are my praise." Others brought food from time to time. Several neighbors drove me to early chemotherapy treatments. Others sent cards. My beautician helped select and cut the best wig for my needs. Another friend who owns a specialty shop for mastectomy supplies, clothing, wigs, and similar needs was a strong shoulder to lean on with her years of experience and insight.

On "Day 17" of chemotherapy, as predicted by my nurse, my hair really started falling out, so I called my sister, long-distance. We chatted away, while I whacked off my hair with scissors, as I did not want to be alone and she understood. Later, my husband shaved my scalp and I was ready to pop on the wig. Another long-distance friend, a cancer survivor, called frequently, to compare notes and discuss things other than cancer—such as our children, and hoped-for grandchildren. Others recommended dietary supplements, books, relaxation practices, or music to encourage, ease, and comfort me. I could pick and choose, accept or not, those which suited me. I describe all these contacts, for I count them all as gifts of grace, all unmerited, not specifically asked for, but gratefully received. They came my way as precious reassurances of a Father's love.

These acts reinforced my opinion about how grace is recognized and measured. Dictionary definitions of grace are both general and specific, and the qualities of grace can be experienced mentally, physically, emotionally, and spiritually. I came to see grace in its varied forms, but its essential spirit could not be separated from an act of kindness.

It was also important to give truthful feedback, without telling everybody everything. Friends and acquaintances are concerned and/or curious about how cancer treatments work and how side effects vary from person to person; it is a great opportunity to share a faith story to those who may have fear in their eyes. If a loved one has died of cancer, folks often are skittish about the whole subject and may find a calm spirit in the midst of a storm to be a wonder. It is a natural way to share one's faith and encourage one another.

Sometimes, giving meaningful feedback can be quite poignant. One day, my supervisor told me that she had prayed that I would not lose my hair. But, I said to her, "Sharon, I am completely at peace with losing my hair for a while. I just consider these side effects to be evidence that the drugs are killing cancer cells. It is okay, just keep praying that the treatments will work." I later learned that her sister had died of cancer ... and she had not lost her hair during chemotherapy.

Although my preferred church music leans toward the traditional, there were several hymns on a "Praise and Worship" tape given to me by a friend, which I played whenever I drove to the hospital for a chemotherapy or radiation treatment. My favorite was a tune by Henry Smith, entitled "Give Thanks." The lilting tune and lyrics seemed to sink deeply into my spirit to both humble and strengthen me.

"Give Thanks"
Give thanks with a grateful heart
Give thanks unto the Holy One;
Give thanks because He's given Jesus Christ, His Son.

And now, let the weak say, "I am strong."
Let the poor say, "I am rich."
Because of what the Lord has done for us, give thanks.

From my first chemotherapy treatment just prior to Thanksgiving 1999 through my final radiation treatment on 5 May 2000, these were the words I learned to lean on. There were days when I ached and hurt from the chemotherapy. There were periods of rebound, when I could attend a big family wedding of precious cousins. Our supper club friends were helpful, caring, and fun. Christmas holidays were simplified. The get-away New Year's trip to Key West with family was rejuvenating, with warm weather and lots of sightseeing. Throughout those months, I kept a journal listing not only blood counts and physician remarks, and nurse Sharon's advice about drinking water and how to avoid constipation due to the drugs. I recorded who sent a book, a card, a meal. One reason for keeping a journal was that I found it more difficult to concentrate. I found it reassuring that friends shared their health concerns with me: one had a scary mammogram, and another had an ovarian tumor. Both friends turned out to be fine, but I did not want to be sheltered from their concerns. Sharing both good news *and* bad news is the linchpin of girl friendships. Always an avid reader, I read widely, and discovered passages from Kathleen Morris's searcher's heart to be both interesting and refreshingly expressed in *The Cloister Walk* and *Amazing Grace: A Vocabulary of Faith.*

We celebrated the end of treatments with a dinner at a wonderful five-star restaurant. I wrote thank-you notes to people who helped me and to let them know that we had made it through the treatments. Now the challenge for me, as it is for all those experiencing cancer treatments, was just moving on, monitoring closely for five years with lots of follow-up appointments, hoping and praying that there would be no recurrence. Every yearly mammogram, every blood test or scan, can be anxiety producing. Every doctor's check-up, sitting in the waiting room among patients with varied problems, keeps me grounded in reality. But then, the report is good, and I move back into my new normal zone. Yes, there is no returning to the old normal. Things are never the same; the experience changes a person, as it should. I hope that I am a more sensitive, grateful person.

One of the challenges of mid-life is life review. Six months of cancer treatments certainly ensured that this was accomplished. I am more likely now to act on any inner urging to call, write, or share a word of encouragement. Simple pleasures are more satisfying and more important. Hearing the voice of my daughter is more precious. The joys and challenges of the years since 2000 have included surviving and recuperating from injuries in a car wreck, retirement, aging parents, and becoming a grandparent, which, hopefully, I have met with a faith and patience tempered by that episode of cancer. Being human is a chronic condition, and the best treatment for this condition is a nurturing faith in Christ; we are nourished and then can reach out to others. Our focus should be upward and outward. Self-absorption leads to depression, drudgery, dullness, and isolation. By seeking to try an attitude of gratitude, and by looking for acts of grace, my faith and spiritual life grew deeper and my friendships grew sweeter.

The Goodness of God

Melvin T. Jackson
Senior Pastor
Calvary Baptist Church
Pittsburgh, Pennsylvania

It has been said that when life gives you lemons, you should make lemonade. But, what about when life serves you a death sentence? What about when life tears you down and fills you with sorrow? What do you do? Where do you go? Who do you turn to? What answers are there when you don't even understand the question?

Well, I believe that the only one you can call on and cling to in times like these is God. I submit this chapter of one of my life's experiences to render a word of faith to anyone who needs it to get through hard and difficult times.

Some may say, "Why me?" But I say, "Why not me?" Why, it's my story. I must say simply, as I recount this story, that God can do for you what he did for me. The fact of the matter is that I'm glad I even have a story to tell; I'm glad that I was chosen to be used, so that I could become useful through telling my story.

Where do I start? Well, I guess I should start at the beginning. I must add up front, however, that it's not how one starts out; it's how one ends up. I would like to thank all those who were responsible for giving me this opportunity to give a portion of my life's experience.

It started about ten years ago when I was faced with the most frightening experience of my life. I had no expectation or anticipation of what could happen, how it might happen, or how it would develop.

In August 2001, I was invited to spend twelve days in Wiesbaden, Germany, to be a part of a Baptist convention. The convention was designed to bring pastors, preachers, deacons, and ministry leaders together to teach and preach to the Baptist congregations in Germany. I was blessed to be invited to be a part of that contingency from across the nation, with a mission to go to Germany and service the people (many military personnel) with teaching, preaching, training, and church administration.

Prior to my going to Germany, I had a physical examination. My doctor saw a lump on the left side of my neck; it was about the size of a hazelnut. There was no pain or discomfort; however, I was losing weight. I wanted and needed to lose some weight. Being six feet, four inches tall and weighting 275 pounds, I carried it well; however, I still could stand to lose a few pounds.

After seeing the lump, the doctor suggested that I get checked out upon returning from Germany. There were no worries in my mind and no real concerns because I was healthy on the outside; however, unknown to me, there was a problem I could not see on the inside.

Upon my arrival in Germany, I met a preacher by the name of John Harris from New Jersey. We befriended one another and became very close. As we shared pleasantries, he told me he had just gone through a bout with cancer—squamous cell carcinoma of the neck. His lump had been cancerous and had required surgery and radiation, but he was now on his way to complete recovery. The story he told me was so intriguing that I admired his struggles and his overcoming. Little did I know that within the next two weeks I would be faced with the same disease as John Harris.

When I returned to the states, without any knowledge of my current condition, I went to the doctor and was referred to a specialist (oncologist), and was diagnosed with stage 4 cancer of the neck. The prognosis was as follows: surgery immediately, followed by radiation, five days a week for six weeks, then chemotherapy.

The most frightening statement after the evaluation was that I would be faced with was the possibility that I would never talk again. Being a preacher, this was the most devastating report I could ever receive. But I resolved myself to the fact that I serve a God who is able to do all things, exceedingly and abundantly beyond all that I could ask or think.

It was the most difficult thing I have ever experienced. I lost all of my hair, my skin turned jet black, and my teeth were completely decimated from the radiation. From just one dose of chemotherapy, I lost 130 pounds. Chemo infected my entire body, and I was in intensive care for fourteen days to deal with the spreading infection in my body. They placed a feeding tube in my stomach, projecting I would need it for one year, but I refused to use it. I just pushed myself to eat orally in spite of the pain in my throat.

I was then placed in a nursing home with the prognosis that I would not be coming home. I was on a morphine drip to help manage my pain. To aid the healing process, I was placed in a hyperbaric chamber five days a week for six weeks. This was to increase the number of red blood cells that would aid the healing process. I was not able to preach for one year, three months, fourteen days, twelve hours, and thirty minutes.

The question is: How am I today? Well, I'm so glad you asked.

I'm back in my pulpit. I now weigh 215 pounds. I have regained my stamina; the cancer is in complete remission; I am stronger, wiser, and better than I have ever been in my life.

I owe the credit to God alone, and will forever be indebted to my lovely wife minister, Thelma Jackson, who stuck by me, not part of the way but all of the way. When I wanted to give up, she made me get up. When I wanted to give in, she slapped me back to reality. When I felt lost and alone, she told me she loved me too much for me to give up on God and her.

The irony of this saga is that God was with me all of the way—from Pittsburgh, to Germany, back to Pittsburgh, through the surgery, through the radiation, the chemo, the pain, the suffering, and the thoughts of it being the end.

My journey was simply like this: I went to a country I had never been before, met a man I had never met before, to tell me of a disease I didn't know I had, to prepare me for something I had never gone through, to come out of it all doing more than I have ever done before to serve the kingdom of God.

Everybody has a story, and my story is "Blessed assurance Jesus is mine." I pray that my story will inspire someone to never give up. No matter what your eyes may see or your mind may think, never give up on God because he is able to make all things perfect.

Looking the "Big C" Straight in the Face

John E. Chowning
Vice President for Church and External Relations and
Executive Assistant to the President
Campbellsville University

As a baby boomer, born in 1951 during the height of the Korean conflict and the waning months of the Truman administration, my life has been, for the most part, one of positive experiences, hard work, and commitment to Christ and family. I had the opportunity to grow up on a farm in southern Kentucky in a stable and loving Christian family, and to attend small-town schools. My brother and I were encouraged to work hard, go to college, stay active in the community and church, and prepare for professional careers.

Cathy, my wife of forty years, and I met during our freshman year of college and were married between our sophomore and junior years. Both of us settled into successful career paths and were blessed with the births of four children. We moved to Campbellsville, Kentucky, in 1977, and our roots run deep in this part of the Commonwealth. Despite a few bumps along the way, with my wife's diagnosis with melanoma in 1977, the loss of a baby in 1980, and a few ups and downs that all people face, we enjoyed successful lives and became well established in our careers, church, and community. In the early 1980s, I felt a call from God to become involved in bivocational pastoral ministry and entered into that new phase of Christian service.

Several opportunities came my way in the 1980s and 1990s in my secular career, including my involvement as a partner and vice president of a consulting firm. In addition to my ministry and family obligations, I traveled extensively in Kentucky as part of the business and became very active in civic organizations and politics. Life was good, our children were growing up, and my wife's career was going well. Needless to say, the pace of life had increased significantly, and a few health issues began to become apparent: low back problems, hypertension, allergies, and other typical middle-age maladies. It seemed that the more I did, the more I was asked to do and the more I needed to do.

The "Big C" Hits

Looking back at 1993 and into 1994, I can see a pattern of increasing fatigue and stress. I kept going at a rapid pace and became even more involved in my secular and church work and civic and political activities. Plus, a few years prior, I had begun to serve on the board of trustees of then Campbellsville College, a Baptist-affiliated liberal arts college. This affiliation would prove to be an important life experience for me in just a few years.

In the summer and fall of 1994, I began to feel even more fatigue and varied aches and pains. One Sunday evening in November 1994, following a full day of church services and activities, I discovered a sudden and extensive swelling of lymph nodes. Aware that this was potentially symptomatic of something very serious, I canceled an out-of-town trip on Monday morning and saw my primary care physician that very day. We discussed the full range of possible conditions that the symptoms might indicate, from various kinds of infections to some type of malignancy.

Over the next month, I underwent a series of medical tests while taking a series of powerful antibiotics. Several doctors told me that I obviously had an infection of some kind. However, I became convinced that my condition was something more serious.

After discussion with my primary care physician, a decision was made for me to undergo a CAT scan at our local hospital. By this time, I was generally prepared for the conclusion of the radiologist that I was dealing with a type of lymphoma. Within a few days, I was back at the hospital to undergo surgical biopsies to arrive at a final medical diagnosis—or so I thought.

The surgeon, oncologist, and pathologist concluded that we were dealing with lymphoma, a type of non-Hodgkin's lymphoma (NHL). The prognosis, from their perspective, was somewhat mixed, and suddenly I was listening to discussions of myriad treatment possibilities, including different regimens of chemotherapy, radiation at some point, and eventually a stem cell transplant. While I was prepared emotionally and spiritually for the diagnosis of cancer, I was pretty much overwhelmed by the range of options mentioned and the underlying hint of limitations on long-term survival. We arrived home in a state of exhaustion, and while we maintained a positive outlook, we were scared and overwhelmed. The "Big C" had arrived in our lives, and I was only forty-three years old. This could happen to someone else across town, but not to our family. We honestly confessed such thoughts as: "Why do we have to deal with this, Lord? We've been faithful to you, so why us?"

Contending with Initial Diagnosis

Considering myself as a well-informed person and one who is able to deal with the reality of the moment, I was ready to move forward after a day or so of prayer, family discussions, and recuperation. At my request, the staff of the hospital delivered to me the latest information available via the National Cancer Institute's Physician Data Query (PDQ) on the full range of NHL types, treatment protocols, survival, and related data. A hard copy of the PDQ was necessary at that point in time since we did not have home Internet access in 1994. It was my goal to become as well versed as possible on the subject of NHL, while consulting with oncologists on optional treatments.

Since I lived in a small town and led a relatively high-profile life in the community, the news of my cancer diagnosis spread like wild fire. In a matter of days, it was widely known in the Campbellsville-Taylor County community and beyond. That was a mixed blessing. On the one hand, we received numerous phone calls and visits from family and friends, colleagues, and our church family, expressing concerns, offering prayers for healing and strength, and sharing words of encouragement. On the other hand were others who offered expansive words of wisdom and advice, those who looked at me with pity as if I were already gone, and those who shared with me their own knowledge of others who had died with NHL. I recall phone calls from two different widows who shared with me that their husbands had both died with NHL and that they were "so very sorry." I remember another woman who later told me that she "couldn't believe how bad I really did look."

To those who may read these words, please remember that it is not necessary to offer to newly diagnosed cancer patients words of wisdom, great pronouncements on why such things happen, or comments about death to come. Cancer patients are fully aware of the seriousness of the condition and the possibilities of what looms ahead. What they need are words of encouragement, a hug or gentle acknowledgement of concern, a brief phone call or visit, a card or note in the mail, an e-mail or text message of hope. The "Big C" has hit the person and his or her family, and the patient knows how serious and ominous a cancer diagnosis is.

In a small town, the vast majority of people mean well. They are truly concerned about their neighbors. Churches of all denominations placed us on their prayer lists, and we truly felt the prayers of the Christian community locally and around the world. The patient is somewhat numb at times and is dealing with a range of emotions and physical disabilities, so the prayers of God's people are empowering and critical in the recovery process. At the same time, people like to talk, and by the time the news of my diagnosis had made its rounds, the cancer had allegedly spread to my bones and brain and had been declared inoperable. Now, I can look back on those rumors of my imminent demise with a smile and in the knowledge that most people were truly concerned when making those comments and repeating the rumors.

Medical Decisions

Once the shock of the initial diagnosis was past, the time came to find the best medical team and course of treatments. I was immediately faced with a series of important choices: determining where to go for treatment, selecting the oncology team that was best qualified, and agreeing to a protocol of treatment that offered the best hope for survival. Given my desire to be well informed and involved in the medical decisions to be made, I was in store for a bumpy ride.

My first official oncology visit did not go well. The Christmas holidays were nearing, I was anxious to get treatment under way, and I was appalled when two oncologists entered into a debate in front of me as to the particular protocol to be followed. It was an eye-opening situation and one that reaffirmed my inherent feeling that this was not the place for me to be for treatment. I returned home, contacted my primary care physician, and chose to consult another oncologist; that proved to be the right choice in the years ahead.

The diagnosis of NHL is not an easy process, given that there are numerous types of the disease resulting in very fine distinctions between variant types. Five pathology reviews were required prior to pinpointing the final diagnosis. Once the final diagnosis was made, a specific chemotherapy regimen was selected. The next several months of treatment into mid-1995 became a blur of increased fatigue and some complications from the treatment. This became a time of prayer, reflection, and spiritual growth coupled with an ongoing schedule of treatments, tests, and consultations.

During this time, I decided to divest myself of some business interests and began working on a part-time basis with US Representative Ron Lewis, a good friend recently elected to Congress. My volunteer work with Campbellsville University increased as I served on its board of trustees as vice chairman for two terms and then as chairman for two terms as the institution was entering a strategic period of growth and development. By late summer 1995, I was able to work full-time for Rep. Lewis, and I was beginning to return to a relatively normal routine. My church family at Saloma Baptist Church, where I had served as pastor for more than a year, was very supportive, and I was able to fill the pulpit most every Sunday.

I would later realize that God was clearly moving in my life as I experienced a much closer walk with Jesus Christ and sensed the leadership of the Holy Spirit in a clear and direct manner, more than ever before. God was using this experience to clarify my calling to ministry and to direct me in a path of service that became very important. In addition, I acquired an even deeper clarity on what it means to have hope in Christ and to truly live the full, abundant life that he came to give us.

An Unexpected Event

In the fall of 1995, I had my first CT scan following the completion of chemotherapy a few months before. Cathy and I were not prepared for the results. We received the news that the NHL was growing, and I was in need of a much more aggressive type of treatment. My remission was short-lived, and a team of doctors with whom we had consulted (my oncologist and I had decided to confer with this medical team at another hospital in case of a relapse) following my chemotherapy, recommended moving quickly to a much more aggressive treatment, basically high-dose chemotherapy with a stem cell transplant. This was described as my best chance for longevity. Without the prescribed course of treatment, my life expectancy was not particularly encouraging. After some prayerful consideration, I began the pre-treatment, which included several days in a major medical center. After then returning home for a few days, I checked into a cancer center in early December for an extended period of treatment and stem cell infusion.

I checked into the center in early December 1995, expecting to be there for several weeks, but I soon found that my expectation of being an informed patient and having my questions answered forthrightly by the medical team ran counter to the head of the medical team's demeanor and approach. One evening, literally just a few hours before the final phase of high-dose chemotherapy was to be administered, the doctor and I came to a point of no return. He told me he did not have time to respond to my questions. I found that totally unacceptable and informed him and the staff of my decision to go home. While some might consider my decision rash, I was at peace with my decision and fully cognizant of the risks to my health involved in checking out of the hospital and returning home that evening. My immunity was low as a result of the chemotherapy I had received and the advancing rate of the NHL. But there were fundamental issues at stake in this situation: I had to be at peace with my decision on medical treatment, and I had to have trust in the medical team. I simply did not believe that this was the right course of treatment to pursue. And, more importantly, I was at peace spiritually about what was ahead.

The next morning, I called my regular oncologist, who had treated me the first time, and told him of my decision. I am forever grateful to this particular doctor who understood my need to be informed and to have my questions answered. He recommended a relatively new chemotherapy, developed originally to treat a type of leukemia, which had been given temporary approval in treating my type of NHL. Over the next six months or so, I underwent a series of treatments, and I encountered a number of complications along the way, including a major blood clot, viral infections, and shingles. With God's grace, a lot of will power, and the support of family and church friends, I was able to work during this period and led a relatively active and normal life. And, I survived.

Conclusion

The treatment worked. I have been in remission since the summer of 1996. My condition is technically incurable, but God is good indeed. I was able to work for nearly two more years with Rep. Lewis, continued pastoring, enjoyed watching my four children grow up and move on in life, and joined the administration of Campbellsville University as vice president for church and external relations and executive assistant to the president, where I continue to serve. My current work and involvement reflect the many experiences and opportunities I have undergone during my life: serving as a pastor, working at a fine Baptist university, leading in racial reconciliation ministry, staying active in a number of organizations improving the quality of life and economic and educational opportunity for all people, helping our four children become adults and secure good educations and career paths, enjoying the blessings of a wonderful wife for forty years, being amazed at how incredible our four grandchildren are, and experiencing an appreciation for each day as never before.

First Peter 3:15 challenges us: "Always be ready to make your defense to anyone who demands from you an accounting for the hope that is in you" (NRSV). Space limitations preclude a full commentary on this verse. Suffice it to say that my experience with cancer has helped me to contemplate the meaning of this verse with a deeper level of understanding. My doctors have affirmed that a part of the healing process lies in the mysterious nature of the Christian faith, in the power of prayer, in the determination to move forward, and in maintaining a hopeful attitude. As a result of my cancer experience, I am more aware of the need to share the hope that I know in Jesus Christ.

The experiences of the past seventeen years have helped me better understand what Jesus was sharing in John 10:10b as he spoke of his coming so that we might have a full or abundant life. Our call is to live each day to the fullest, to be thankful for that day, to focus on our family and friends, to minister to the "least of these" (Matt. 25:45), and to savor the moment. God did not cause my NHL, but he has used it to help me refocus my commitment to him and to my fellow human beings.

In addition to thanking God, I would like to say thanks to my wife, Cathy, who has stood by me faithfully through these and other experiences. Our four children (Kacey, Emily, Kaleb, and Laura) and our four grandchildren (Jacey, Jacob, Haley, and Kenzi) are the joys of our lives. We are grateful for the love and support of the wonderful saints of Saloma Baptist Church. My colleagues at Campbellsville University, including President Michael Carter, are an amazing and talented group of professionals who are working hard to provide quality Christian higher education. Their prayers and support are appreciated. Dr. Douglas Feltner, my primary care doctor, and Dr. John Gohmann, my oncologist, are tributes to their professions.

Thanks to these and many other friends who have stood by us these many years.

Index